# The Ultimate
# Italian
## Wine Tour

### pocket Guide

A Simple Guide to the Best Italian Vineyard Experiences, from Tours and Tastings to Choosing the Right Trip for You.

by E.V. Luther

I
♥
Italy
.wine

# THE ULTIMATE ITALIAN WINE TOUR POCKET GUIDE

A Simple Guide to the Best Italian Vineyard Experiences, from Tours and Tastings to Planning the Best Trip for You.

by

E.V. Luther

I ♥ Italy.wine

Copyright © 2023 by DiSH Creative Ltd

All rights reserved.

No portion of this book may be reproduced in any form without written permission from the publisher or author, except as permitted by U.S. copyright law.

# About I Love Italy.Wine

The Iloveitaly.wine group is a small and perfectly formed bunch of friends powered by wine and the flowing conversations and excellent life decisions it brings with it. We tour the supermarket aisles and wine regions of Italy and undertake wine courses and classes to bring our digestible wine knowledge to readers who are also looking to make smarter decisions... on wine; of course, we can't help with it all.

Notwithstanding the gloriousness of many other alcoholic beverages, in all its majesty, wine has no competition, and the desire to learn more and choose wisely has united us as friends and experts. We hope this book takes care of the geography of wine, gets you through a dinner choosing a decent one with a date, and does a pretty good job on some of the grape and culture stuff. Enjoy, and cheers! Follow us on social media @iloveitalywine

# About this Book

This is the second in the *ILoveItaly.wine* instalment of fun and facts about the world of Italian wine. As if our previous wisdom wasn't enough already, we are back this year with the next book in our series - the ultimate guide for wine enthusiasts looking to explore the vineyards of Italy in person. From the rolling hills of Tuscany to the picturesque landscapes of Piemonte, this is the perfect handbook to take on the trip, but also beforehand to learn the journey ahead of the most iconic and historic vineyards in the country. That old saying still applies to the best holidays - if you fail to prepare, you prepare to fail.

The book begins with a short introduction to the history and culture of Italian wine, including an overview of the different grape varieties and wine-making techniques used throughout the country. We don't spend too long on this as, ideally, you have the extended version of this from the first book, The Italian Wine Connoisseur. It's a shameless plug if I say so myself, but genuinely, it saves on doubling up.

It then goes on to explore the different wine regions of Italy, including Tuscany, Piedmont, Veneto, and more - and has dedicated chapters for each specific region including the best local vineyards, wineries and wines. It will tell you how and when to visit, what you can expect to find from the experience, and which groups of people each may suit.

The book includes our trusty hand-drawn maps, photographs where possible, which we credit at all times, and practical information such as opening hours, making it easy for readers to plan their own vineyard tour. We also have snippets of interviews with winemakers, wine experts and sommeliers, who share their credited knowledge and insights on the local wines and culture, giving readers a deeper understanding of the traditions and practices of the regions.

With "The Ultimate Italian Wine Tour Guide. Your Pocket Guide to Exploring Italy's vineyards" in hand, readers can plan their own tour of the country's most famous vineyards and discover the secrets behind the production of some of Italy's most iconic wines. This book is a must-read for anyone planning a trip to Italy's wine country or those interested in wine, travel and Italian culture.

# Contents

1. Introduction to Italy's Wine Regions — 1
2. The Wine-Making Process & History in Italy — 31
3. Things to Know by Regions: When, Where & How to Get There? — 63
4. Tour of Northern Italy's wine regions — 105

Please review this book! — 153

5. Tour of Central Italy's Wine Regions — 155
6. Tour of Southern Italy's Wine Regions — 211
7. Wrap-up — 261

Please review this book! — 265

References — 267

## Chapter 1

# Introduction to Italy's Wine Regions

A wine tour in Italy offers a unique chance to experience the country's incredible scenery and culture whilst enjoying the finest Italian wine and food at the same time. For those who are looking for the wine trip of a lifetime, whatever that looks like for you and your group, this is the perfect environment to choose. And it is no ordinary wine tasting - it's some of the best in the world.

In this book, we share our research, memories and favourite recommendations for Italian wine tours, the wineries themselves, and even some of their best bottles to take you to all corners of this unique wine-making country. Whether you are drawn to the rolling vineyards and Renaissance splendour of Tuscany as a group of friends ready to splash the cash, or you are looking for the rural adventures of Sicily with your partner on a romantic wine break (steady on), we will do our best to share our finest ideas for an unforgettable trip. This will involve many of our favourite vineyards where we will share our preferred red, white, sparkling and dessert versions - and we will be with you through the fun of trying everything in between!

Italy's wine country is a perfect destination for wine lovers looking to expand their wine knowledge and improve their home cellars' collections and their horizons of wine tasting, all at the same time. Millions of people every year, including us lucky *IloveItaly.wine* folks in the name of research, make their way to many of the 20 beautiful Italian wine regions to enjoy unique and personalised wine tourism experiences. Wine tourism in Italy is based on long-lasting traditions of winemaking and winemakers being able to share with tourists the enthusiasm for production like nowhere else. This friendliness and kindness of culture are complemented by amazing food, rolling landscapes and landmarks scattered across the country to enjoy along the way.

We will take you through the best vineyard and wine experiences we have been lucky enough to experience ourselves or those we have heard about by word of mouth and want to share with those who are lucky enough to get there before us! We can promise memorable experiences and a warm welcome from those wineries and wine routes we recommend - but more importantly, some incredible wines to try!

Italy is one of the largest wine-growing countries in the world, and this is the most exciting time to explore. Wines come from 20 wine regions (more of that next) that are popular far beyond their borders and are exported all over the world for our drinking pleasure.

This is because the wines themselves are incredibly diverse, with a nearly equal balance between red and white varieties, all being produced to exceptionally high standards. The broad Italian selection of wines appeals to a wide range of cultures and tastes, making them popular worldwide. Italian wines are particularly well-suited to complement the flavours and culinary traditions of Mediterranean cuisine, which is adored by many and why lots of us flock to Italy. Their seamless integration of wine with vibrant and beloved Mediterranean dishes enhances the overall dining experience we cherish. *(Wine Tourism, 2022)*

## Wine Regions of Italy

So, for anyone not well-acquainted with the maps in our last book, "The Italian Wine Connoisseur: 7-Day Guide to Mastering Italian Wine", we are providing the information again now, to make it as easy as possible to understand and visualise the 20 wine regions of Italy - never an easy feat. The wine regions are diverse and authentic, representing different and unique winemaking traditions and heritage.

A revisited list of the 20 regions is below, and we will cover a selection of these that stand out for specific charm and well-known wine production:

1. Piemonte

2. Tuscany

3. Veneto

4. Emilia-Romagna

5. Lombardy

6. Sicily

7. Abruzzo

8. Trentino Alto-Adige

9. Campania

10. Puglia

11. Friuli-Venezia Giulia

12. Sardinia

13. Marche

14. Lazio

15. Umbria

16. Calabria

17. Molise

18. Basilicata

19. Liguria

20. Aosta Valley

# THE ITALIAN WINE TOUR POCKET GUIDE

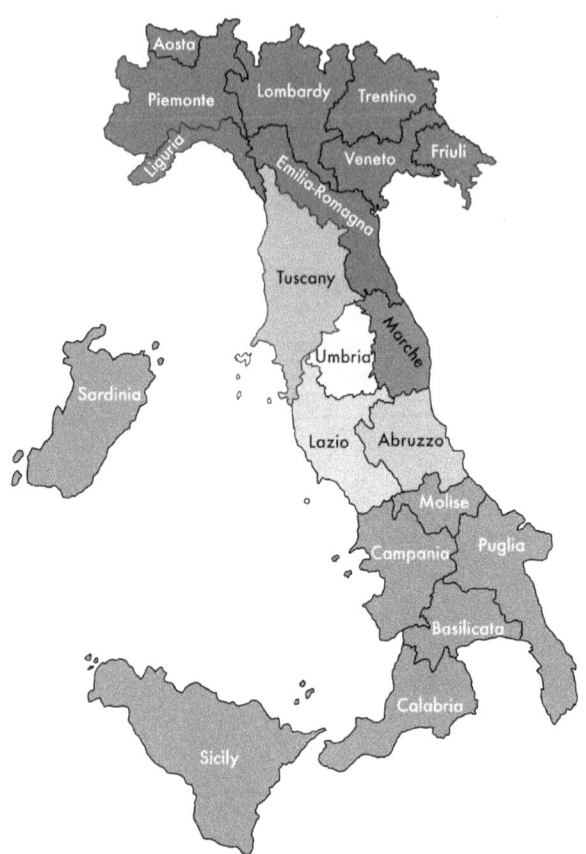

*Figure 1. Italy's Regions*

Now, my map-loving friends, breaking down each of these regions properly with map guidance will follow soon in Chapter 3, but for now, I want you to be able to envisage the general geography and know what each region provides if you want to skip to a specific region. I won't tell. Each region has its own unique characteristics, reflecting the climate, soil, and winemaking traditions of the area (and they can vary greatly).

This is known as the wine's 'terroir'. For those of you still traumatised from my first book's description of this term, to quickly recap, 'terroir' is a term used in wine terminology to describe the environmental factors that influence the character and quality of a wine. These include the soil, climate, topography, and many other geographical features of the vineyard where the grapes are grown, which affect the resulting wine. Because each of these impacts the way the grapes grow and, therefore, the flavours and aromas they develop, this is an important characteristic and is often referred to as the reason for the uniqueness of wines to their terroir.

Winemakers use this knowledge about a wine's terroir to much greater effect - they use the area to make decisions about grape varietals, growing practices and wine-making techniques that will help maximise the grapes' potential and produce their best wines. Italy's division into these administrative regions can be split even further into several wine sub-regions. Still, I will refer to these as 'areas' to keep it as simple as possible.

The most 'significant' of the 20 regions, with both quality and quantity taken into consideration, are Piemonte, Tuscany and Veneto - but we will also look beyond these regions into specially chosen or lesser-known wine regions and their consistently high-quality wines. *(Wine-Searcher, 2022)*

To introduce these wine regions briefly and individually (for those of you with a plane ticket booked and needing the quick version), here is a look at the complete list of the most important wine regions and their unique characteristics, which we explore in-depth chapter by chapter later in the book.

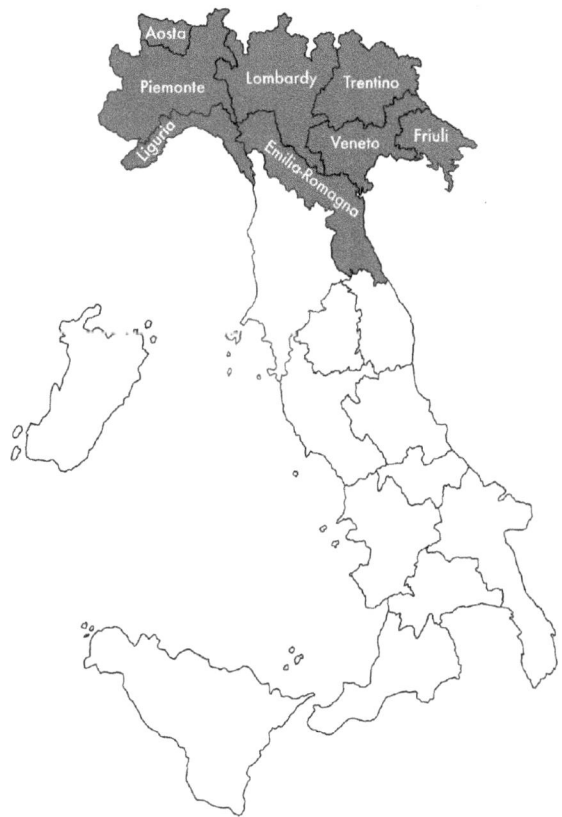

*Figure 2. Northern Italy*

Starting at the top of Italy in the Northern regions, Piemonte in the northwest corner is known for its red wines, particularly Barolo and Barbaresco. These wines are made from the Nebbiolo grape variety and are known for their rich, complex character, with notes of dark fruit, spices and tobacco. The region's wine production is concentrated in the Langhe Hills, where the hilly terrain and cool climate provide the ideal conditions for the Nebbiolo grape. So, if you need to know one spot, head for the hills, and don't take that personally.

Hopping over to Lombardy while still in northern Italy, the region is known for its sparkling wines, particularly Franciacorta. Franciacorta is made using the *Traditional Method,* similar to Champagne, and is known for its crisp and elegant character.

Then there is Veneto, located in the northeast, known for its white wines, particularly Soave and Prosecco - the toast of any great hen-do. Soave is made from the Garganega grape variety and is renowned for its floral and mineral character, while Prosecco is made from the Glera grape variety and is celebrated for its fresh, fruity character and bubbles.

The region's wine production is fairly concentrated in the Veneto hills, where the terrain and moderate temperatures provide a great environment for these grape varieties. We will deep dive into those hilly terrains and everywhere else that may require your best hiking boots together in detail in our first chapter.

Now to the queen of Italian wine regions: Tuscany. Located in central Italy, Tuscany is the epitome of a luxury Italian wine holiday and is a postcard region of rolling hills, making it a stand-out area for winemaking.

Later on, in Chapter 2, we will discover all the main wine-growing areas of Tuscany and its vineyards to visit, from Central Tuscany to the Tyrrhenian Coast.

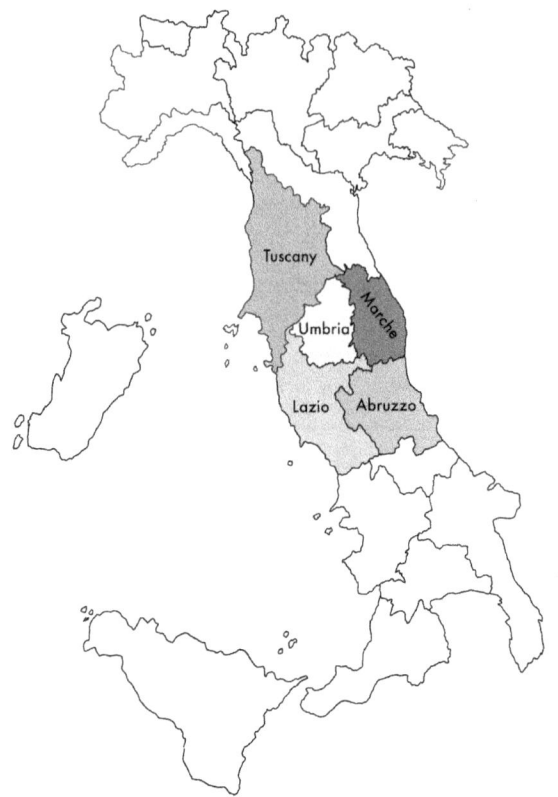

*Figure 3. Central Italy Regions*

Tuscany produces some of Italy's most reputable wines, and many of the names you will frequently hear of are widely produced and well-known, for example, Chianti Classico and Vino Nobile di Montepulciano. For those of you with a bucket list of the big wine labels, we will cover Tuscany in detail and do it justice, I promise. At this stage, if it's top of the list, look no further red-wine lovers than the Chianti, a blend of Sangiovese, Canaiolo, and Colorino grapes.

The wine production area of Tuscany is concentrated in the Chianti Classico area, where the varietal is produced and a perfect setting for the Sangiovese grape.

The rolling vineyards and olive groves are dotted with farmhouses, castles, and cypress trees. So, if you have dreamt of riding a Vespa on Tuscan hills and tasting heavenly wines, then this is not a dream, and we will share everything we know in detail.

Umbria, right next to Tuscany in central Italy, is less well-known or commercial but is also famed for its red wines, particularly Sagrantino di Montefalco. For those who are interested in more unusual wines, do look out for it.

Sagrantino is a grape variety grown in a very limited area in Umbria and is known for its intense and tannic character, with notes of dark fruit and spices - so if you're looking to experience this grape, it's one of the few places you will find it!

Being at the centre of the Roman Empire alongside other central regions, vine-growing in nearby Lazio has been widespread for centuries. But even before the Romans, winemaking began with the Etruscans in Lazio and nearby Central Italian regions.

To give some historical background, the Etruscans were an early civilisation that lasted from the 8th century BCE to the 3rd and 2nd centuries BCE *(Time Maps, 2022)*. In the 6th Century, the tribe expanded their influence over a wide area of Italy, including Lazio - they founded city-states in Northern Italy and even further South. The early city of Rome was deeply influenced by Etruscan culture, and in these central areas, they quickly spread agriculture and winemaking traditions.

Lazio continued to grow vines and produce wine throughout time, but after the pest phylloxera hit the region, as did the rest of the country, Lazio changed their choice of grapes and wines out of necessity. It became known as a 'bulk wine' region, concentrating on quantity over quality. *(La Vita Roma, 2020)*

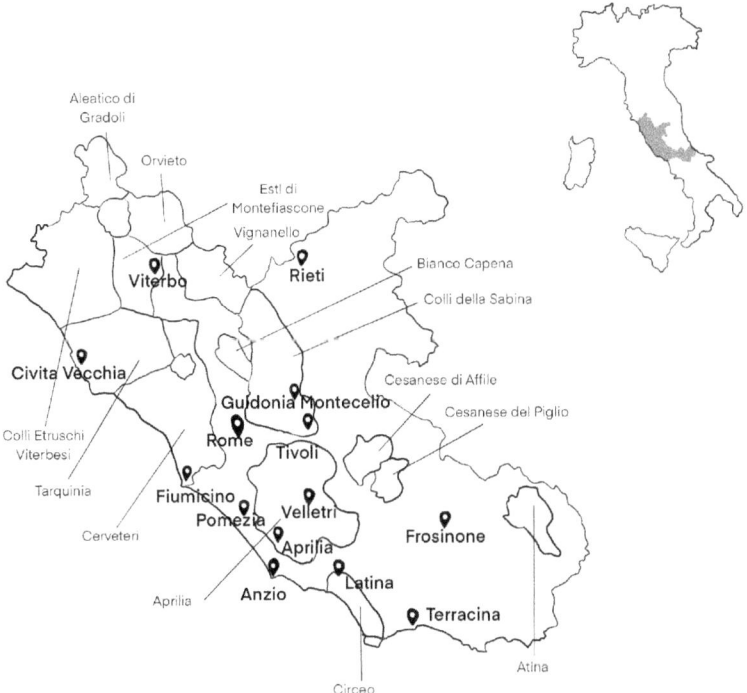

*Figure 4. Lazio Region*

Today, it has shifted its reputation and worked hard to focus again on producing quality wines and become renowned for quality - highlighting native grapes and producing noble international varieties *(La Vita Roma, 2020)*

The Lazio wine scene today is an impressive and easily accessible area for enthusiastic wine lovers, with its proximity to Rome airports and ease of travelling distances. Although we don't cover the region as its own Chapter later in the book, the area is likely to be included in some way during your time if you visit Rome - so it would be rude of me not to provide a basic understanding of the wine scene.

Nowadays, from anywhere in Europe, you could fly to Rome for a city break followed by a few days on a wine tour with the click of a button and only a few hundred euros.

50,000 acres of the land in Lazio are under vines, with about 40% of wine production dedicated to DOC /G designation *(La Vita Roma, 2020)* guaranteed quality wines. You can choose what suits you from these elite designations or the very appealing, more everyday IGT wine areas in the region, which are sprawling and fun to try.

*Figure 5. Fountain at Frascati*

Finally, while in Central Italy, flitting along the Adriatic coast, the region of Le Marche is one I will cover in its own right as a little gem of a notable wine scene that offers diversity and great, lesser-known wines.

Verdicchio is the flagship and most well-known white grape variety here, and one I like to drink enormously while in the UK, as I have recently found that UK supermarkets offer a great selection.

*Figure 6. Le Marche Region*

Wines made from Verdicchio are crisp, refreshing and often characterised by vibrant acidity once those taste buds are finely tuned (I'm here all day!).

Verdicchio dei Castelli di Jesi and Verdicchio di Matelica are two prominent appellations within Le Marche known for producing excellent Verdicchios. If you're there for the red wine instead, then Rosso Conero is a red wine you will find in this pocket-rocket of a region, made primarily from the Montepulciano grape variety.

For such a small region, Le Marche also produces other names like Pecorino and Passerina, which we will jump into properly later, as they have gained recognition in recent years.

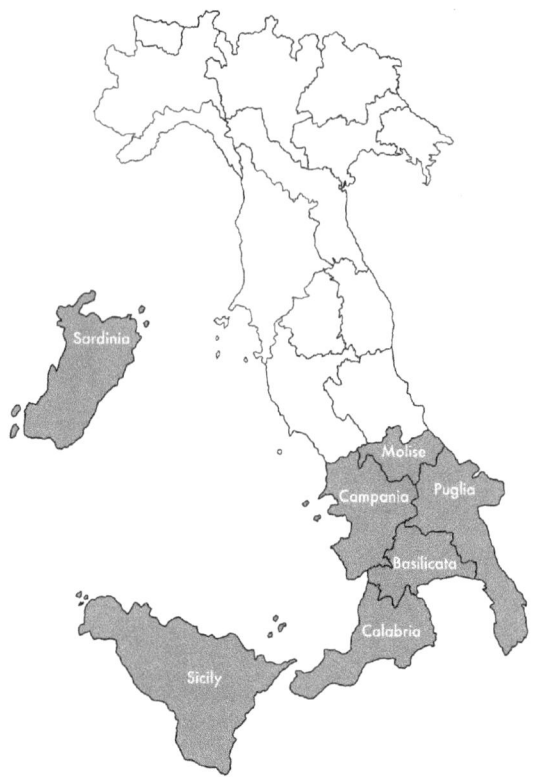

*Figure 7. Southern Regions*

Now, when skipping down to Southern Italy and looking at wineries and experiences in Campania, I must flag that they often include pizza ( and, naturally, I am heavily swayed by this), but tours to the Campania region are a broader topic for discussion - often from Naples as a starting point, so again very convenient for those travelling by plane and with only a weekend to spare.

*Figure 8. Naples and Sorrento*

The hills of Sorrento and the Gulf of Naples are also not a bad backdrop to many of the wineries offering outstanding day experiences. I have found myself in a Campania vineyard one moment, a citrus grove the next and, even then, on a farm tour thrown in for good measure.

An example of a slightly more lowkey wine-tasting experience in Campania would be a demonstration of the wine flight, then a mozzarella and caciotta-spinning tasting, followed by a pizza-making class in a farmhouse, with matched wines and a full guided tour.

Now, looking at the Italian islands, which often get swept into the 'southern Italy' label but are, in fact, a world of wine unto themselves, we look at the islands of Sicily and Sardinia, respectively.

Sicily is one of Italy's most important wine regions, producing a wide variety of wines, from fresh and crisp whites to rich and complex reds. It also happens to be one of the most captivating holiday destinations of all time and where I plan to get married next year, so that doesn't go down badly either.

*Figure 9. Sicily*

As someone who has seen the wave of love for Sicily over the past few years, and I hope by now someone with a level of expertise in Italian wine, I will give an overview of some of the best regions to visit in Sicily and what I recommend you taste, but for now here is the quickfire version:

Mount Etna is one of the most unique wine regions in Italy, let alone Sicily, located on the slopes of an active volcano. The volcanic soil and high altitude produce wines with a distinct minerality and acidity. Other than a volcanic eruption, here you should also look out for wines made from the Nerello Mascalese grape, which is the most well-known variety in the area. We will cover this grape in greater depth in the Sicily chapter and other areas of the island.

You will also want to dip a salty toe into the Marsala region of Sicily, famous for its sweet dessert wine from the local Grillo, Catarratto and Inzolia grapes. This fortified wine is perfect with sticky toffee pudding and not to everyone's taste, but beautiful if you have a sweet tooth - aged for a minimum of two years in oak barrels and has flavours of caramel, nuts and dried fruits. Lastly, we will look closer at Vittoria, a small town southeast of Sicily known for its unique red wine from the Frappato grape.

We visited this area with this wine in mind and found it light and fresh, with notes of cherry and strawberry. Not far from there is Noto, another small town known for its red wines made from the Nero d'Avola grape. These wines are full-bodied and rich, with flavours of black cherry, blackberry, and spice - tours of these vineyards won't disappoint, and we will delve into how best to see it all later in the book.

Lastly, on my *'we've barely got time so I have to choose'* wine regions list, is the magical island of Sardinia. **Sardinia** is an island in the Mediterranean Sea that boasts over 2,000 kilometres of coastline, postcard beaches and hectares of craggy mountains.

The combination of a rugged landscape and the oceanic elements in the soil produce astonishing wines that never taste better than being there in person looking out to sea while wondering which restaurant to choose for dinner. Heaven.

*Figure 10. Sardinia*

Sardinia wine tasting is mainly concentrated to the North and East of the island, so bear that in mind if you want to fully explore the island and plan around it. The superior quality of wines in Sardinia often ensures wine tasting is truly memorable - wineries like Cantina li Seddi, which we will explore in full later, are well-known as one of the best wine tastings on the island and one of the most enjoyable things to do in Isola Rossa.

Moving over to the East, you will find outstanding wineries nestled in the valleys in the eastern part of Gallura, and you can expect to try all types of wines in Sardinia, from Vermentino and Cannonau to Muristellu, Carignano and Cabernet Sauvignon.

The regions mentioned above are just a few of the 20 wine regions making up Italy, each with unique characteristics and specialities, all of which would deliver an outstanding trip worthy of any wine lover. But rather than tackle them all, I will do my best to provide a concise guide to those mentioned for the discerning and savvy wine traveller.

## When to visit?

The next question to address early on is *when* it is best to visit Italy's rolling vineyards or coastal wineries. We do not want to take the blame for not seeing a single harvested grape or for having no sunshine during your long-awaited wine-tasting trip. So, early Spring and early Autumn are ideal times to visit Italy if you hope to explore the wine regions, and in general, it is best advised to take this kind of trip, especially if you want to see the harvest. We will explain why and what different times of the year mean for the winemaking practises shortly.

Firstly, it avoids being in Italy when temperatures are hotter than the Sun, often from June - August. Secondly, as mentioned above, the grape harvest occurs each September and October (exact dates vary from year to year), so the warm start of Autumn can be an excellent time for die-hard wine lovers wanting to see the whole process and enjoy perfect temperatures.

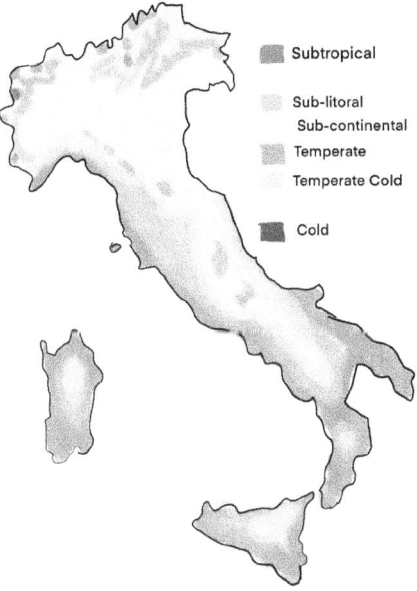

*Figure 11. Weather in Italy*

The benefits of learning about these regions in advance and adopting the knowledge shared in this book are that you can plan your wine-tasting trip with less wasted time and more time sipping!

We hope it allows you to choose the right time to visit, take a logical journey through Italy or a specific region, pick the best winery experiences for your group, and meet some wonderful producers and friends.

You will be able to choose wines more cleverly and base your choices on an appreciation of the grapes and the ageing process - and if you're going to send crates of it back to your home country, it's a good idea to get it right!

You'll never look back once you know your planned tour of Italy. We hope you can rest easy knowing you can refer to this guide whenever you need it before or during your trip.

As you will see, each Italian wine region has its unique characteristics and specialities, making the country a diverse and attractive destination for any wine lover. From the rich, complex Barolo of Piemonte to the crisp and refreshing Verdicchio of Marche for example, Italy's wine regions offer a broad range of wines to suit every palate - so go with what works for you and your group, and don't overcommit too much so you get to enjoy it.

Whether you're a wine enthusiast with years of experience or (more likely with us as your North Star!) just looking to try something new and relaxing, exploring the wines of Italy's regions is always a journey worth taking. We just ask that you take us with you...

Chapter 2

# The Wine-Making Process & History in Italy

The wine-making process in Italy has been passed through centuries, and constantly evolved to where we are today, where wine in Italy is considered as important as food, sunshine and fashion. The introduction of w and vinification to Roman culture centuries ago, helped to develop the economy through trade with neighbouring populations. It spread to Southern and Central Italy, and when the Romans took over, it was exported all over Europe. *(Aveine, 2022)*

Of course, what the Romans consumed is far from the kind of wine we drink today. The vinification process was not very refined, probably with wild and acetic fermentations (oxidation process that turns alcohol into vinegar) happening, which would have led to a clunky end result.

The wines at the time were commonly mixed with water (with a higher proportion of water than wine), milk or honey for sweetness, and this was especially true of the lower-grade, bitter wines.

In this chapter, we will take a closer look at the various steps involved in the Italian wine-making processes we see today that have created a refined, world-famous country of winemaking and the wineries that have shaped Italy in getting there. You will be lucky enough to see the process and the end result bottlings in wineries across Italy, as well as the grape varieties and traditional methods used to produce some of the country's most renowned wine labels.

The methods used will vary across regions and, depending on whether you want to see the generations-old traditional techniques, or new biodynamic wineries adopting innovative practices, will determine the Italian region you choose to explore and what your experience will look like.

*Figure 12. Wine-Making Amphorae*

## Grape Harvesting & Crushing

Grape harvesting is the first step in the wine-making process, and what you will be looking to capture for that essential social media shot of bare-foot, grape-crushing glory.

This stage typically takes place between September and October, so ensure you book for the right time of year. If you visit Tuscany in early September, for example, right at the beginning of the harvesting season, you may coincide with the grape stomping - where many wineries celebrate the very first day of the harvest with an almighty stomping to kick off the season and fermentation of the grape juice. The grapes are hand-picked and carefully sorted to ensure that only the highest quality grapes are used for winemaking.

Now, let's get cultural... a *"vendemmia"* is the Italian word for an authentic Italian grape harvest. *(Arianna and Friends, 2023)* It is one of the most *Italian* of Italian wine experiences you can enjoy and drops you right in the epicentre of the local wine scene and culture. If you long to be in the vineyards during the September-October harvest season, then *la vendemmia* is your time. This will happen in many charming wine estates, where you can see the winemaking process during the most operational phases and taste the excellent local wines over lunch. *(Arianna and Friends, 2023)*

Arianna and Friends (www.ariannaandfriends.com) and other tour companies offer an experience set explicitly in the vineyards with the harvesters at this time of year. Arianna and Friends tour takes place for about two hours (timing is flexible) in the morning, with a local guide who takes you through everything from the planting to the cultivation, as well as the weather conditions of the seasons and how they affect the grapes. *(Arianna and Friends, 2023)* Then, and only then, are you allowed your own clippers and crates before being set loose into the world of harvesting!

*Figure 13. Grape Harvesting*

As is Veneto, Tuscany is a great region to see this, but anywhere at the right time of year, you will have the opportunity to see the grapes being picked and transported to the winery, where they will be processed into wine. You may also have the opportunity to participate in the grape harvesting process, even if you have yet to book a specific experience to do so and get hands-on with the staff, which can be a fun and educational, if not messy, experience. Needless to say, leave your white linen at home.

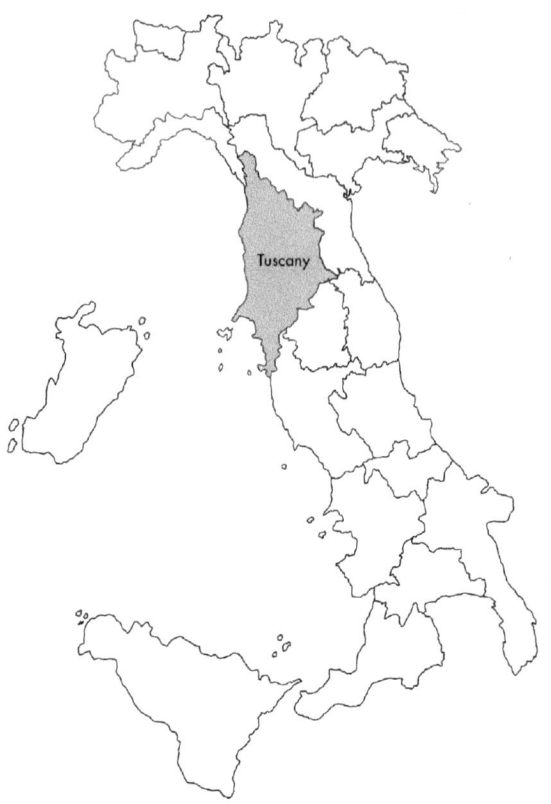

*Figure 14. Tuscany*

It's important to note that not all wineries in Tuscany, or anywhere else for that matter, allow visitors to pick grapes during harvest season. Tuscan wineries that allow visitors to pick grapes during harvest that I know of and can recommend are:

Castello di Meleto is a winery located in Gaiole in Chianti. They offer a grape-picking experience during the harvest season from September to October. Visitors can participate in the picking and sorting of the grapes, as well as a general tour of the castle with wine tasting throughout the year. Set high in the hills, among vineyards and woods, you can explore the gardens surrounding the castle, ancient cellars and the picturesque eighteenth-century theatre even before the clippers come out. The visit will end in the *Enoteca* (Italian for 'wine repository') with a tasting of excellent wines. See more online at www.castellomeleto.it, and for reservations, contact wineclub@castellomeleto.it or call +39 0577 749129

Villa Calcinaia winery is located in Greve, also in Chianti. They also offer a grape-picking experience during harvest season, where visitors can participate in the grape harvest for a day in the sunshine and learn about the winemaking process from expert harvesters. Villa Calcinaia started organic farming in 2000, first on the olive groves, then extending to all the vineyards. (www.conticapponi.it) The organic process is also applied to the small vines used for new plantings and, therefore, involves the nurseries. Here, the more hands on deck, the better to ensure the organic standards are met with no interference. From €20 up to €500 (with Reserva wine vintages included in the price), you can experience several different levels of tours of the winery, tastings and meals. See all options at https://www.conticapponi.it/calcinaia/activities/ and contact them directly about ensuring grape-picking at Via Citille 84 - 50022 Greve in Chianti (FI). Call +39 055 853715 or email commerciale@villacalcinaia.com. The winery is open all year from Monday to Friday from 09:00 to 18:00 (On Friday, it closes at 17:00)

Fattoria La Vialla is a winery in Arezzo, another area of Tuscany. They offer grape-picking, a tour of the winery and a tasting of their organic wines, cheeses, olive oil and almost every other kind of local Italian delight. Fattoria La Vialla is a family-run, organic-biodynamic farm and wine estate, and the type that will make you feel good about the world immediately. It was rescued from abandonment by the Lo Franco Family in 1978. *(Lavailla.com, 2023)*. Today, it is home to organic and biodynamic methods to cultivate 1,600 hectares of land and produces its own wine directly from vineyard to bottle. After being part of that process, it is reassuring to think their precious food and wine goods are not sold anywhere else. You can only order them to your home by ordering online at https://www.lavialla.com/en-GB/orderform/ or your country link or by requesting the catalogue. Here, visitors also taste a variety of wines once bottled, made by your own precious hands, and just a few of the organic varietals that you might get to try include the following:

- Chianti: Fattoria La Vialla produces several different Chianti wines, including Chianti DOCG and Chianti Colli Senesi DOCG - the best of the best. These wines are made primarily from Sangiovese grapes and other local grape varieties. They are typically dry, medium-bodied wines and all are incredible, with notes of red fruit, herbs and spices.

- Vino Nobile di Montepulciano: This is an organic version of the red wine made from Sangiovese grapes grown in the Montepulciano region of Tuscany. It is a full-bodied wine with notes of black cherry, tobacco and leather.

- Vernaccia di San Gimignano: This is an outstanding white wine made from Vernaccia grapes grown in the San Gimignano region of Tuscany. It is dry and crisp with notes of citrus and almond.

- Vin Santo: This sweet dessert wine made from Trebbiano and Malvasia grapes will finish the wine tasting perfectly. The wine is a deep amber colour with dried fruit, caramel, and nuts flavours.

*Figure 15. Chianti and Pecorino Toscano Cheese*

In addition to these wines, Fattoria La Vialla also produces other organic varietals, such as Rosso di Toscana IGT, Bianco di Toscana IGT, and Super Tuscan IGT. The exact wines available for tasting may vary depending on the season and availability - and look into these before going if you want more than to help crush the grapes.

Contact the winery at +390575430020 / email fattoria@lavialla.it / WhatsApp +393316108627 or Skype on: call_lavialla

Additionally, across all of the Italian wineries sharing access to the grape harvest, you can learn about the history and culture of their regions and the winemaking process from the staff. It's important to note that the availability and timing of grape-picking experiences may vary depending on the winery and the weather conditions during the harvest season. It's always a good idea to check with the winery to confirm availability, get your weather apps out, and book your experience with the hope of some good luck and sunshine on your side.

*Figure 16. Red Wine Grapes*

After the grapes are harvested, they are crushed and, like white grapes, are pressed to extract the juice at this stage. The grapes can be crushed using traditional methods, such as foot treading or modern techniques, such as mechanical crushers, which are also impressive to see if you haven't before.

The juice is then separated from the skins and seeds in a process known as pressing. My friends, this is the 'crushing and pressing' stage- if only life were so simple.

Like with harvesting, if you're a wine lover visiting Italy hoping to incorporate seeing the crushing and pressing of grapes, it's best to know that not all wineries offer this insight, so plan ahead. You must align with the same time as the grape harvest - ideally September and early October. Later in the book, I will go into finer detail about many wineries by region. Still, several regions and wineries offer this experience specifically, so look out for them. Here are a few suggestions of those I know that welcome guests to observe the crushing and pressing stages:

- Piemonte is a wine region in the north-western part of Italy known for its high-quality red wines - cue the map in the previous chapter again for reference. Some of the wineries in the area that offer grape-crushing and pressing experiences include Marchesi di Barolo, Fontanafredda, and Vietti - details about specifics can all be found online.

*Figure 17. Piemonte*

- Veneto is the wine region in north-eastern Italy famous for its sparkling Prosecco wines. Go here for the bubbles and grape harvesting in the area, slightly earlier in the year due to the terroir (usually between August and September). Some of the wineries in the area that offer grape-crushing and pressing experiences include Bisol, Nino Franco and Ruggeri. Again, look into the exact details online and book the right timing for you as a group.

*Figure 18. Veneto*

During your visit to these wineries, and any other letting you in on the process, you can admire as the grapes are carefully harvested and transported to the winery for crushing and pressing.

You can also participate in the process, helping sort and crush the grapes. Think of picking the best ones for your fruit salad, and we'll be onto the right level of attention to detail. This can be an excellent opportunity to learn about the winemaking process, how your favourite wines are produced, and see the whole supply chain.

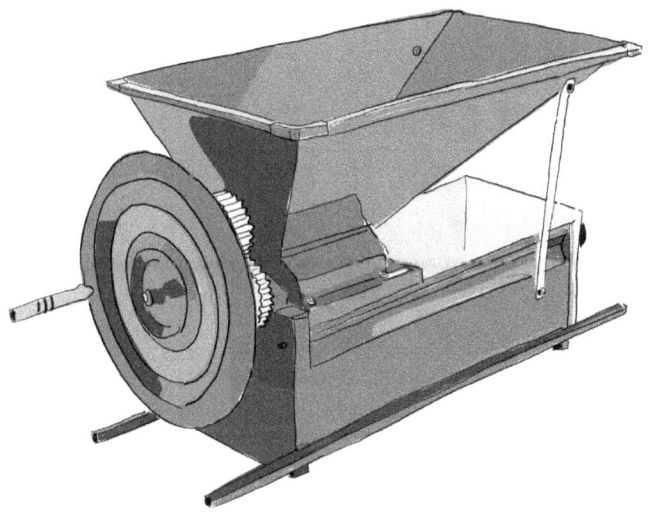

*Figure 19. Grape Pressing Machine*

## Fermentation

The next step in the wine-making process is fermentation, which converts the juice into wine. After crushing and destemming, the harvested grapes in modern-day wineries are commonly put into the fermentation vats, which may vary in size from 50 to 5000 gallons. *(Tuscany Tonight, 2022)* These vats are where the alcoholic fermentation of the grapes takes place, which is carried out by yeasts, consuming the sugar in the juice and releasing alcohol and carbon dioxide as a by-product.

Fermentation can also occur in stainless steel tanks or oak barrels, depending on the type of wine produced and the common practice of the winery. Most red grapes go to the fermenter before pressing for primary fermentation (the above process of converting sugar into alcohol and CO2). In contrast, most white grapes are just pressed before fermentation. Some white grapes are fermented in small oak barrels for added aroma and flavour, and at that stage, the yeast is then added to the barrels for fermentation. *(Tuscany Tonight, 2022)*

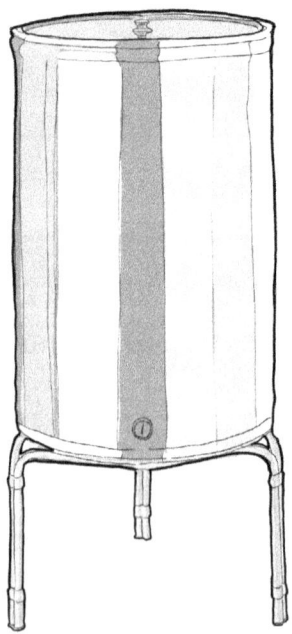

*Figure 20. Fermentation Stainless Steel Tank*

After fermentation, the wine is aged to develop its flavour and complexity. This process can occur in stainless steel tanks, oak barrels, or underground caves. The type of ageing and the length of time will depend on the type of wine being produced and what region of Italy you are in. During your visit to these wineries, you can see the barrels and rooms where the wines are aged, learn about the different methods of ageing and their impact on the final wines, and as with all worthwhile winery visits, sample the aged, fine wines.

Southern Italy is a great place to see ageing wines, and regions that, although not internationally considered as poster-child for the Italian wine scene, offer just as much in this regard. Several regions and specific wineries provide the experience of digging deep and seeing the ageing process and the more personalised stages of winemaking. Here are a few suggestions of areas we have tried and tested to see the ageing process and a closer look at how it is achieved:

- Campania in southern Italy is known for its rich and complex red wines, such as Taurasi and Aglianico del Taburno. Many wineries in the area have underground cellars where the wines are aged in oak barrels for several years, and you can visit these. Some wineries to consider visiting are Feudi di San Gregorio, Mastroberardino and Mustilli, which we cover later in the book.

- Puglia is a wine region in southeastern Italy known for its bold and flavourful red wines, such as Primitivo and Negroamaro. Many wineries in this area have similar cellars, which you are also welcome to explore. Some wineries to consider visiting include Cantine Due Palme, Fatalone and Leone de Castris for great, famous aged wines.

- Finally, our great love, Sicily - off the southern coast of Italy, is known for its diverse range of wines in all shades. Some wineries to consider visiting for the ageing and barrel process on the island include Planeta, Donnafugata and Tasca d'Almerita.

## Ageing

As the wine ages in the oak barrels you stroll among, it takes on the flavours and aromas of the wood and the flavours of the previous wines that were aged in the same barrels for generations. This process is called "micro-oxygenation" and helps to create a unique flavour profile for each type of wine, It is certainly part of what gives Italian wines their charm and a piece of rich history and traditions.

When the wine has reached the desired level of ageing, it is carefully removed from the oak barrels and bottled - you may also see this at some wineries, and we will point out those wineries specifically later when it applies. The result is a complex and flavourful wine enhanced by the ageing process in oak barrels.

*Figure 21. Ageing in Barrels*

After ageing, the wine is blended to create a consistent flavour and style - this is particularly important for wines made from multiple grape varieties or from different vineyards and act as a 'Nutribullet' of the grape world.

## Bottling

The final step in the wine-making process is bottling. Hallelujah. The wine is filtered, blended, and bottled under a vacuum to protect it from oxidation. During your visit to wineries that allow you to see and help with the bottling lines, you can see the stage where the wines are carefully bottled, labelled and packaged.

At this point, you will learn about the different methods of bottling and labelling and how the winery ensures the quality and consistency of its wines before being sent out for distribution.

Bottling wine in Italy involves several steps, including filtering and preparing, which means even before bottling, the wine is prepared to ensure that it is free of sediment or impurities. Then, the wine is transferred from large tanks to individual bottles filled to the appropriate level - no guessing game is involved here.

Finally, the corking and labelling mentioned above, with information about the wine, including the producer, vintage and grape variety per Italy's appellation system. (I hope you remember that from our previous book?)

In Italy, wine is typically bottled at the winery or specialised bottling facilities. So if the wineries in your region don't offer an insight into bottling, it might be worth hunting out the bottling facilities that do. These facilities often handle the bottling needs of multiple wineries, providing a cost-effective and efficient way to package wine - so perhaps less wholesome and picturesque to see but undoubtedly practical when wineries get to a specific size.

*Figure 22. Bottling*

In many wineries in the Veneto area, we have seen bottling lines where the wines are carefully bottled and labelled with guests during their wine tours.

Some wineries to consider visiting in Veneto include Marchesi di Barolo, Vietti and a winery many of you may know the bottling well already - Gaja.

Once bottled, Italian wine is exported to many countries worldwide, hence how many of us know it so well. The main destinations are the United States, Canada, the United Kingdom and China, among many others, all of whom have come to love and appreciate Italian wine labels as some of the most popular in Europe for exportation.

## What to See and Do on a Wine Tour

If you're heading on your Italian wine holiday outside of harvest time, there are still plenty of options for experiencing the country's rich wine culture and having, let's face it, a total ball at any time of year with a glass in your hand and the Italian sunshine beaming down on you.

The basic premise of what you see and do during the other months in wine territory is *winery tours* and/or *wine tastings*. Think less Australia and New Zealand 'cellar door' type winery experiences (for those of you from there or have tried those, also simply fabulous, of course) but more a pre-booked, orchestrated, planned day that is bookable in advance and often with a small to medium-sized group that includes lunch and pairings.

Many Italian wineries offer tours of their vineyards, cellars and production facilities at any time of year. This can be a great way to learn about winemaking and see where your favourite or brand-new wines are produced.

The wine-making process in Italy combines traditional and modern techniques, as mentioned before, reflecting the rich winemaking traditions of the region and embracing constant evolution.

The diversity of grape varieties and methods used makes the Italian wines unique, and each winery experience is different, giving a wide range of options for wine lovers and the happy wine-drinker group to choose from. Anywhere you go on a tour, you can expect to learn about the history and culture of the winery and the region the different grape varieties and winemaking techniques used to create the final product.

At wine tastings, you get what it says on the tin as your main takeaway - to *try* the wines first and foremost. A tasting is a great way to sample different wines, normally logically from their palest, citrusy whites all the way through to their darkest, plummy reds (if a red *and* white producer) and learn about their unique characteristics and flavours, as well as the process they have undergone.

Think of this as a less active version of a tour but equally as friendly and knowledgeable.

Many wineries offer tastings of their wines accompanied by complimentary local foods such as cheeses, cured meats and bread - so you can tick off lunch simultaneously. If others don't, you can likely select a platter once there and enjoy your own bottle of wine afterwards. You can also learn about the different grape varieties and terroir that give each wine its story.

Some of the best wine-tasting experiences in Italy I have been on and recommend before we even deep dive by region include those guided in a tasting room. You can also participate in food and wine pairing experiences, where you will learn how to pair the different wines with delicious local cuisine one can only dream of recreating at home. Furthermore, many estates also have a wine shop selling local products and wines, like olive oil, balsamic vinegar and cheeses.

No matter where you go in Italy, there are endless opportunities to experience the country's rich wine culture and sample some of the world's best wines in a tasting experience. Whatever region you choose, you're sure to come away with a deep appreciation for the art and science of winemaking and some seriously good wine under your arm.

## Grape types

Now, onto the grapes themselves. As we covered in our previous book, *The Italian Wine Connoisseur: a 7-day Guide to Mastering Italian Wines*, Italy is home to over 2,000 grape varieties, each with unique characteristics and specialities. Some of the most important grape varieties used in Italian winemaking, which you are likely to come across according to region, include:

*Nebbiolo* is a grape variety grown primarily in Piemonte and used to make some of the most renowned wines in Italy, such as Barolo and Barbaresco. However, you will undoubtedly see it elsewhere. The grape variety is known for its rich, complex character, dark fruit notes, spices and tobacco.

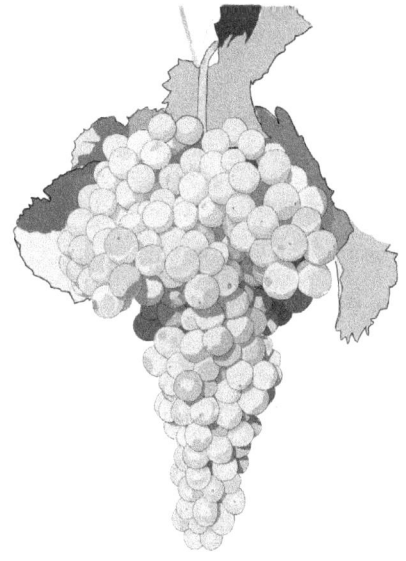

*Figure 23. White Wine Grapes*

Other grapes you will probably already know the names of and would be right to look out for throughout Italian wine country include *Sangiovese*. This grape variety is grown primarily in Tuscany and is used to make some of the big wine names in Italy, such as Chianti. The grape variety is known for its red fruit character, with notes of cherry, plums and spices.

*Aglianico* is a well-known grape variety grown primarily in Campania and Basilicata in Southern Italy and is likely to cross your winery path if you explore the South. It is used to make some of the most renowned wines in southern Italy, such as Taurasi and Aglianico del Vulture, which are known for their complex character, with notes of dark fruit, spices, and tobacco.

Native to Southern Italy, specifically to the regions above, it makes bold, tannic red wines that are often compared to Barolo or Nebbiolo - and be sure to head to the areas of Taurasi and Irpinia, where it is the primary grape variety used in the production of Taurasi DOCG wines, the best of the best.

If you are interested in tasting Aglianico wines, the above nuances suit you, you can visit wineries well-known for producing Aglianico wines, including Feudi di San Gregorio and Mastroberardino in Campania and Paternoster and Elena Fucci in Basilicata. These two regions are your go-to; you will have a wonderful holiday.

*Garganega* is a well-known grape variety grown primarily in Veneto and used to make some of Italy's most renowned white wines, such as Soave. The grape variety is known for its floral and mineral character, and if you're keen to hit up your whites, you will find many. If you want to see the Garganega grape variety in Veneto and also visit the wonderfully captive city of Venice as well for example, then a few places certainly worth noting to factor in them both include:

- Soave is a town in the Veneto region about 30 kilometres east of Verona, which is also well worth visiting and known for producing white wines from the Garganega grape. You can visit Soave's many vineyards and wineries to learn more about the grape and the winemaking process and be in Venice in a couple of hours by train for a few extra days of city break.

- Monteforte d'Alpone is a small town located in the province of Verona known for producing the Soave DOC white wine. Vineyards surround the town, and you can take a tour to learn more about Garganega at all of them.

*Figure 24. Venice Grand Canal*

Venice itself, with its canals, architecture and art, offers everything we already see and hear about this magical city - landmarks such as the Grand Canal, Saint Mark's Basilica and the Rialto Bridge - either all by gondola if your feet are tired from all the vineyard tours or by foot if you still have it in you.

Overall, the wider Veneto is a beautiful region to explore with wines in mind, but it also offers a rich history and culture to your trip, world-class cuisine and great photo opportunities.

We will look at many more grape varieties as we explore every wine region in detail in this book. The wine industry is highly fragmented and has the largest indigenous grape varieties of any country and many small-scale producers. *(Aveine Paris, 2022)*

This means that Italy offers one of the largest varieties of wines and that there is a huge diversity in grape types and how they are grown. What's more, Italian grapevines are cultivated in every one of the 20 regions and at every altitude *(Aveine Paris, 2022)* and vineyard extension has reached massive new heights in the new wave of winemaking.

The above are just a few key grape names to get your head around or for those who have heard enough to book their tickets already, for everyone else, we will look at signature grapes and grape families as we explore regions from North to South within the book.

In addition to utilising various grape varieties, Italian winemakers rely on traditional methods to produce some of the country's most renowned wines. Some of the most essential traditional methods you are likely to see and should consider before planning your wine journey include:

- *Sfuso* is a traditional method of bottling wine in large glass containers, typically between 20 and 40 litres each. This method is used to produce some of the most renowned wines in Italy - such as Chianti. The large containers allow the wine to age and evolve naturally, but you'd certainly need patience on your side as a producer.

- *Amarone* is a traditional method of winemaking used to produce a unique style of wine from the Veneto region described above. The grapes are left to dry on straw mats for several months before being pressed and fermented, and this is a unique version of winemaking you will have to be in this area to find. This process concentrates the sugars and flavours in the grapes, resulting in a wine with high alcohol content and a rich character.

- *Barrique* is a traditional method of ageing wine in oak barrels - as noted previously. This method produces some renowned wine types in Italy, such as Barolo and Barbaresco. The oak barrels impart a unique flavour and complexity to the wine, often adding notes of vanilla, spice and toast, depending on the exact oak type.

Needless to say, cast your wine net wide and be open to the type of trip and tasting experience that might suit you. I will take you through how I, like many visitors, arrive in a region of Italy for the wine itself, and in this sense, the wide selection never fails to disappoint.

But depending on where you choose, you can also enjoy other experiences there: a city break, a dip in the sea, moments with nature or scenic hikes stretching for miles. So, depending on what you want to do around your wine-tasting experience, I hope to share the best of each region outlined and take you on our own tour before you do it for real!

## Summary of Chapter 2

I hope this chapter has given you a helpful overview of the various steps involved in wine-making and what you can expect to see in wineries across Italy depending on the time of year, the size of the operation and what processes you may get to see. We have also covered the major grape varieties and the traditional methods commonly used to produce some of the country's most renowned wine labels.

We have shared the production stages from grape harvesting to bottling and where it is best to have a personalised, beyond-the-scenes experience of these stages should it be your priority. Otherwise, I have started introducing plenty of options for experiencing the country's rich wine culture at any other time of year and covering the 'wine tasting & tour' packages at different times of the year and what these terms mean.

As for grapes, I have suggested you choose what suits you best or those you have enjoyed before - as you will smell, breathe and taste them every day you are wine tasting. In this chapter, I hope I have also done justice to introduce the warmth of the Italian winemakers and their heritage estates, who consistently deliver authentic experiences and their Italian family charm.

I hope you plan not just a wine-tasting tour but a banger of a life experience and an insight into the passion and history behind winemaking in the local Italian regions I love so much.

## Chapter 3

# Things to Know by Regions: When, Where & How to Get There?

As a writer appealing to those planning a wine tour of Italy, I thought it would be helpful to pull together a list of do's / dont's and helpful pointers on what, when and how to plan the perfect trip - basically everything you wished you knew in advance and usually learn the hard way. I will include information that may be helpful regarding the best times of year to go, the most popular wine regions to visit, how to make the most of them, and pricing trends.

As mentioned above, the 'best' time to visit Italy for a wine tour, generally speaking, is often presented as the peak season for wine tourism, which is the fall (Autumn) harvest season, from September through to November time. This is when the grapes are harvested and the wineries are bustling with activity but is also dependent on the region you plan to visit for the exact best weeks within this period. However, the summer months, from June to August, are also popular times to visit and needless to say, especially for those who love the sun, (shamelessly, me) and want to enjoy the warm weather and other outdoor activities.

The earlier Spring months, from March to May, are an excellent time to visit if you don't like it as hot, or want to avoid the school holiday hike in flight prices, and the vineyards are already teeming with life.

While the Autumn harvest season is doubtless the most popular time for wine tours in Italy, and the few months around this time above, the winter months are less explored. They can also offer a unique and enjoyable wine tourism experience for those looking to beat the crowds and those happy to pack a light puffer jacket. There are some genuinely great wine tour areas in Italy to consider during the winter months, especially those not tied around dates for children and University holidays etc, for example:

- **A Barolo and Barbaresco Wine Tour:** The Piemonte region in Northern Italy is home to Barolo and Barbaresco wines which we explore in detail later. But before that, I want to let you know that winter, in general, is an excellent time to visit this region, as the vineyards are dormant and the wineries offer cosy indoor tastings with a hearty, classic Italian cuisine to pair with the robust red wines. In fact, it makes even more sense somehow with a fire lit inside!

- **The Amarone Wine Tour:** As we know from the previous chapter, the Veneto region is known for producing Amarone, a dry red wine made from partially dried grapes. Winter is a great time to visit this region, as the wineries offer tastings in the warm indoor cellars, and again you can pair your wines with hearty winter dishes like risotto and polenta for the ultimate winter or festive experience.

- **Chianti Wine Tour:** The classic and famous Chianti region in Tuscany is known for producing some of Italy's most famous and high-quality wines - a big part of the next Chapter to follow.

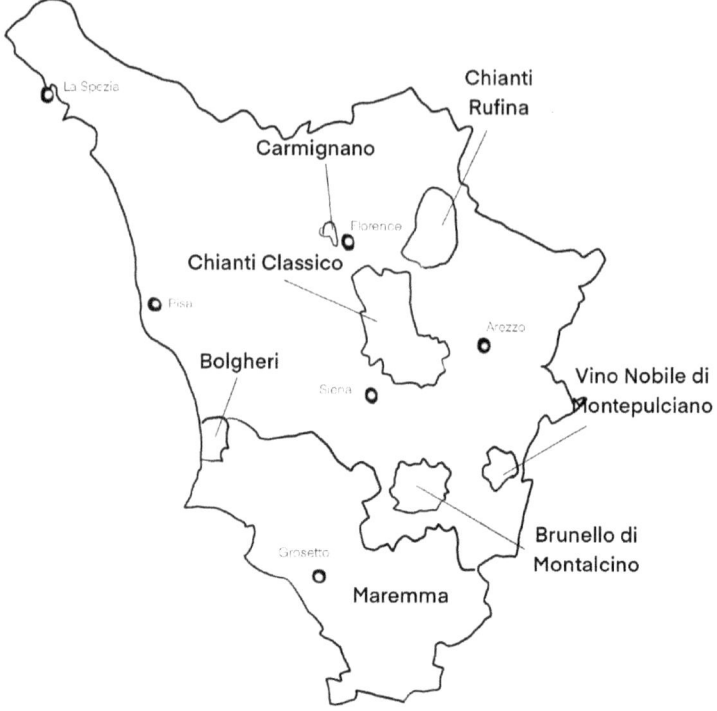

*Figure 24. Chianti Region*

During the winter months, however, an area of this calibre is well set up for a high volume of guests and a great experience. You can enjoy tastings of Chianti wines in the cute tasting rooms and cellars of all the big Chianti wineries we share in this book, as well as take in the beautiful winter scenery of the Tuscan countryside.

- **Valpolicella Wine Tour:** The Valpolicella region, again in Veneto, is known for producing a range of red wines, including Amarone and Valpolicella Ripasso. During the cold months, you can still enjoy tastings in the warmer restaurants of the wineries, and while there, please visit our friends at Carilius Wines, producing the most outstanding Valpolicella Ripasso! You can contact them at CARILIUS VINI, Via Poiano, 25. Loc. Bure - 37029 S. Pietro In Cariano VR. *Email:* info@carilius.it *Phone number:* +39 045 6800563

*Figure 25. Valpolicella Region*

Overall, there are many wine tours in Italy to enjoy during the colder months, and these are just a few examples. Each region has its unique wines and winter experiences to offer, and many are still open, offering a cosy version of the harvesting months, but expect more of the tastings by the fire pits rather than those out amongst the vines, as those my friends, will be looking fairly sad!

On the other end of the scale, if you are planning a wine tour of Italy in the height of summer, either as a fellow sun-lover or needing to align with school holidays or annual leave, then you might want to consider the islands of Sicily and Sardinia over the sweltering mainland during the months of July and August - even the Italians flee from Rome and the other big cities during these times when temperatures are often 35c every day and anything active can feel rather draining.

The Italian islands offer a unique and different experience compared to the mainland, especially during the summer months, and you will certainly keep cooler and be closer to a dip at the beach at the end of a long, hot day.

Aside from the idyllic beaches, of course, there are some things that Sicily and Sardinia offer during the summer months that you may not find on the mainland as easily - local festivals, for example. Both islands have a vibrant and unique culture, with many festivals and events taking place during the summer months. In Sicily, the Festival of Saint Rosalia is held in the island's capital, Palermo, in

July, while the Fish Festival is held in the coastal town of Sciacca in August. In the winter, mid-November, Sicily hosts the Festa di San Martino in Catania, a festival of wine tasting no less, with street food stalls and traditional sweets. *(Just Sicily, 2023)*

In Sardinia, the Festa di Sant'Efisio is a colourful religious procession that takes place in Cagliari in May, and the La Notte della Taranta music festival is held in the town of Melpignano in August. All of these are unique and truly Italian cultural experiences that you could time to perfection on any given year if you want to tie in your island experience with the buzzing wine scene. Both islands also have a rich history and unique architecture, with influences from Greek, Roman and Arab cultures. In Sicily, you can explore the ancient ruins of Agrigento, the Cathedral of Monreale and the seriously beautiful town of Taormina, which many of you will have heard of. In Sardinia, you can visit the ancient ruins of Nuraghe and the stunning city of Cagliari - I went in 2017 and can safely say they love a festival in and out of season as it was September when I visited, and weekend celebrations were the norm!

The islands are also perfect if you are searching for the specific wine types found there - in Sicily, the Nero d'Avola grape is widely cultivated and produces bold, full-bodied red wines, while the Catarratto grape is used to make crisp, refreshing whites. In Sardinia, the Cannonau grape is the most widely planted and produces rich, fruity red wines. If these are names you know and love, head directly to the islands and get your fix whether or not summer floats your boat - every pun intended, boats are plenty on both islands. We will cover both islands as individual wine regions at length in our Southern Italy chapter later in the book and dive into the wine experiences they offer no matter what time of year you choose.

## Italy's Wine Regions and Which to Choose

Now let's talk about the 'popularity' of Italy's wine regions - it's the elephant in the room that Italy has many famous wine regions, but its flagships are without question Tuscany, Piemonte, and I would say Veneto too, which all fall into this category.

Tuscany and Piemonte are two of the most expensive regions to visit (while others like Umbria and Puglia are generally more affordable and at the other end of the scale.) Luxury wine experiences in Tuscany and Piemonte can range from a few thousand dollars or GBP to tens of thousands of dollars or GBP, depending on the specific itinerary, accommodation options, the group number and those additional extras that we all let slide on holiday, but in these regions can really push the boat out and the budget up - extra cooking classes, truffle hunting, hot air balloon rides and spa days for example. Yes, please.

A few of the tour companies that would offer experiences in these regions include Abercrombie and Kent. They are a UK-based award-winning luxury travel company that creates tailor-made escapes - including a Tuscany Food & Wine tour for 7 nights starting at £4,180 per person. During the week-long tour, you take in

Chianti Classico, produced in the hill vineyards between Florence and Siena, and the city's renaissance in both Florence and Pisa. The chance to learn some culinary secrets with private cookery lessons and guided vineyard tours with exclusive wine tastings is included. See more information on the website or by calling +44 1242 386 464 *(Abercrombie and Kent, 2023)*

Generally, luxury high-end wine tours in these regions will offer high-end accommodation, private transportation, exclusive vineyard tours and tastings, and even access to limited-production wines, all as part of the 'package'.

Expectations of the trip would be tailored to the travellers' preferences, which is part of the luxury and what you pay for. It could include visits to world-renowned wineries like Antinori, based in Florence, Tuscany, with vineyards in Chianti Classico such as the above, or even Bolgheri and Montalcino; or Sassicaia winery, located in the coastal region of Maremma, in the southern part of the region. In Piemonte's case, the equivalent luxury level of wine tour might well include those at well-renowned wineries, including Gaja, in the Barbaresco area of the Piemonte region, specifically in the town of Barbaresco in the Langhe hills. Or Vietti, also located in the Langhe hills in the town of Castiglione Falletto. But let's be clear: in these regions, there are plenty of options for high-end winery hopping, which will depend on the tour company and their relationships with certain wineries.

This type of trip appeals to those with a passion for wine, food, and luxury travel and who have a budget to match. Both Tuscany and Piemonte are the pinnacle of wine tasting and experiences, and the sky's the limit for personalisation or making it a once-in-a-lifetime experience - while some may be lucky enough to make it a recurring trip and stock up the wine cellar at the same time.

Now, for a more humble Italian wine experience, there are many affordable wine tours in Italy, and the cost can vary depending on the region, the number of wineries visited, and when you go, as covered in the previous chapter. But in general, it is fair to say that some of the most affordable wine tours in Italy can be found in the regions of Puglia and Umbria, with all their charm. These regions are known for producing high-quality wines at more affordable price points.

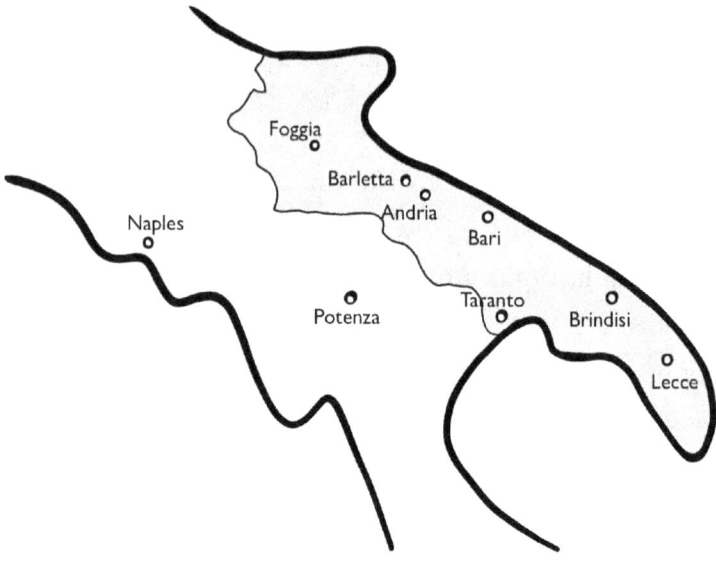

*Figure 26. Map of Puglia*

We will share in later chapters more details on each of these wineries to check out - but for now, some great ones to know about that appeal to big groups of friends on a budget in these regions include Cantine Lorusso in Martina Franca, Puglia - which offers tours and tastings of their Primitivo and many other wines for a small fee, and includes a tour of the vineyards and cellar. Contact them at +39 080.4313309 Or email info@ipastini.it and the website.

The same can be said of Cantina Albea in Castel del Monte, Puglia - which offers tours and tastings of their version of the same wine types, both starting at approx. €10 per person. The winery is located on Via Due Macelli 8 - Alberobello, and contact is by phone at +39 080 4323548 or email at albea@albeavini.com and on the website.

In Sicily, where I have hopefully not under-sold any of its charms, the island also offers affordable versions of wine tours (as if it didn't have everything else already) and high-end versions. Cantine Barbera in Marsala, for example, offers tours and tastings of their Marsala wines for the same sort of price as the above and also pairs your wines with local pastries and desserts.

Run by female winegrower Marilena Barbera, the winery is governed in honour of her father's dreams in Menfi, Sicily. The wines here are made by biodynamic farming and via natural winemaking, and the fiercest girl power and respect to Menfi's terroir. It prides itself on using no herbicides or synthetic fertilisers. Here, you will get time with Marilena herself and feel like part of the family - she excels at spontaneous fermentations and proudly loves to share her unique Sicilian native grape varieties and the beautiful land to which they belong.

Then, at Cantine Florio, also in Marsala on the island, this chic winery offers tours and tastings of their fortified wines and includes delicious local snacks alongside. The guided tour of the Florio Cellars, for €20 per person, does everything a simple, fun wine tour should - starting at the giant vats and onto the barrel chambers beyond, under 104 arches of history. *(Duca. it, 2023)* After a thirty-minute tour through the barrel vaults, you get to enjoy the avant-garde tasting rooms named Donna Franca and Duca Enrico. Tour "Marsala Gourmet", as it is known and bookable, is a visit to one of the oldest wineries in Sicily, trying three quality Marsala Florio wines for less than the price of an average Italian lunch. Florio Winery is located at Via Vincenzo Florio 1, 91025, Marsala, and you can book directly for your exact date and time. Side note: Small pets are welcome if you can carry them, so hello. They are the perfect option for dog lovers!

*Figure 27. Cantine Florio Marsala Wine*

Moving to Central Italy, there are also pockets of great-value wine tours and tastings. The Umbria region, for example, is a charming, lesser-known pocket rocket of a region that produces high-quality wines at a more affordable price point. This means that wineries here are less crowded than those in more popular wine regions, if that is something that suits you, and often offer more personalised experiences. You will also find that many of the wineries in Umbria and similar regions are small, family-owned operations that provide authentic and intimate experiences. Visitors can often meet the winemakers themselves and learn about the winemaking process firsthand.

Umbria is known for its unique grape varieties, such as Sagrantino and Grechetto, which are not widely planted in other regions of Italy. It offers great value for wine tours because of its lesser-known status rather than because it needs more wine quality. So enjoy high-quality wines and personalised experiences without breaking the bank - think of those experiences where you end up having a life-long pen-friend in a host you stayed with for two nights - that's what you can expect here.

Wineries such as Di Filippo in Trevi (possibly the cutest place on the planet) offer tastings of wines such as their Sagrantino, Montefalco Rosso and Grechetto, with all of the wines paired with local cheeses and meats.

Imagine more of a Noah's Arc of happy animals rather than just wine and food here - it is an agricultural gem of a place, built on respect and love for its resident animals as well as the produce. *(vinidifilippo.com, 2023)*

Set in 30 hectares overlooking Assisi, on the hills between Torgiano and Montefalco, it is an understated heart of cultivation which respects nature to the extent that the family and workers have combined the love for their work with quality production in four hectares of vineyard run completely by draught horses, treading the ground between the vines. *(vinidifilippo.com, 2023)* So, trying delicious wines here for as little as €15 for the experience will include meeting the real heroes of the day - and yes, they all have names - horses Dora, Flaminia and Maya *(vinidifilippo.com, 2023)* who, for a very reasonable € 35 will even trot tourists around the vineyard by horse and cart, to show you just how well they do it compared to machinery.

If luck is really on your side, you might even get to meet Sebastian, the latest arrival, Maya's son. And at this point, we would be crying with joy. That's all I'm saying.

The address for Di Filippo Azienda Agraria s.s. Is Vocabolo Conversino, 153, 06033 Cannara (PG) Phone +39 0742 73 12 42; Whatsapp: 389 87 28 282 or email info@vinidifilippo.com There is a dedicated email address for wine tasting options and various food pairings at degustazioni@vinidifilippo.com.

Another great option in the Umbrian gem-scape is the San Marco winery in Montefalco, which offers tours and tastings of their Sagrantino and Montefalco Rosso wines starting at approximately €18 per person.

Antonelli San Marco is an organic winery and farming estate located within Montefalco's DOCG wine-making area in Umbria, and again, you feel the attention to organic practices at every turn here. The resident Antonelli family is passionately committed to caring for their territory and dedicated to producing quality wines as well as extra virgin olive oil. Add to that homemade chickpeas and, for non-vegetarians now, cured pork cuts made from their free-range, happy pigs.

The "Cucina in Cantina" programme was launched in 2009 - a taste education programme specialising in wine tasting and guided cellar visits, cooking lessons, wine-pairing lunches and dinners, open by reservation only. Experience the taste of authentic Umbrian home cooking paired with the right wine. Choose from a 4-course lunch/dinner menu of €50,00. Or a 3-course lunch/dinner menu €35,00. Alternatively, experience a wine cellar visit & tasting of 4 wines accompanied with a bruschetta and extra virgin olive oil. The cooking school, "Cucina in Cantina", is about Umbrian home cooking. A hands-on approach is favoured. The experience includes a tour of the vineyards and cellar and a similar tasting of four wines paired with local bread and olive oil.

Also, for €15, in the area of Montefalco, you can book the Bocale winery experience to see the family-run estate with a member of the Valentini family themselves, who will tell you the secrets of work from the vineyard to the transformation of the grapes. Here, they walk you through their process and the natural wines they produce. From £15.80 per adult.

These are just a few examples of great-value, friendly wineries in Puglia, Sicily, and Umbria, which I have chosen that offer affordable wine tours and tastings from the many more available all over the country. It's always a good idea to check the winery's website or call ahead to confirm prices and availability in these cases, as many will be smaller operations with specific opening times and offerings to groups depending on size.

## Booking Your Dream Wine Tour Experience

There are a few different options for booking a wine tour in Italy. You can book directly with the wineries or through a tour operator specialising in wine tours. The tour operator option is less '1990 travel agency' than it sounds, and many are great, reliable companies still relevant to Italy's current wine country climate. Tour operators that specialise in wine tours can offer a more comprehensive experience, including transportation, meals, and visits to multiple wineries, all organised for within a single day or across several days.

If you are time-poor and don't want to have to arrange these details yourself, then it's a good option. It is also a good idea if Italy is totally new to you and you're a nervous organiser of details like transportation in a foreign country or if you have a large group who are tricky to rally or arrange price-splitting with.

Although booking with a wine tour company or agency will offer a more comprehensive and hassle-free experience, there are still a few things you should know before booking:

- Research the company properly: Before booking a tour, it's important to research and read reviews from other travellers or, even better, go with trusted word-of-mouth from friends or family who have used the tour company before. Otherwise, look for companies with good ratings and reviews online and check if they are licensed and insured.

- Check the itinerary carefully: Make sure the tour itinerary includes the wineries and experiences you are interested in and want to visit. If you have specific wineries or regions you're keen to see, make sure they are included in the price plans, or otherwise, look for ones that do.

- Extras included: Before booking, check to see if meals, transportation, and other activities are included in the tour price and ensure you are happy with the arrangement. Also, confirm what additional costs you may incur at the end of the tour.

- Be clear on group size: Find out the maximum group size for the tour and the average group size. Smaller group sizes can often provide a more personalised experience but are often more expensive.

- Confirm all tour details: Make sure to confirm the date, time and meeting location for the tour in advance. Nothing is worse than missing the meeting spot for the tour departure on day 1.

- Finally, check the cancellation policy: Be aware of the cancellation policy for the tour company. Some may offer full refunds if you cancel within a certain time frame, while others may have strict cancellation policies, and you're pretty stuck if you are outside of this.

None of these are meant to worry you, my friends - they are all tips to make sure you use the right company and do your research in advance. Overall, I personally think booking with a wine tour company in Italy can be a great option for those who want a hassle-free and comprehensive experience; cue busy working mum organising a girls' wine weekend. Or those in big groups and to avoid the faff of splitting costs.

However, following the above, confirming the details and understanding the cancellation policy before booking is important. These tours will range in price depending on the level of personalisation and exclusivity of the experience.

Some popular tour operators for wine tours in Italy include The Wine Bus, Wine Tours in Tuscany and Italia Dolce Vita, but many much smaller ones focus on specific regions. The three mentioned are all well-known tour operators, two focusing on Tuscany.

The Wine Bus is a popular tour operator that offers small-group tours to some of the region's most famous wineries. There are many different options of wine experiences that cover multiple different regions, including Sorrento, Naples and Positano as starting points - and many of which include a city day and/or other experiences. The various tour options are available at https://www.thewinebus.net/. They have received positive reviews from customers who praise their knowledgeable and friendly guides (you'd hope so) and their well-organised and enjoyable tours. The downside? Some customers have noted that the tours can be a bit rushed and that there is limited time to fully explore each winery, so note that if you want a more leisurely experience. Queries are made by phone to the Wine Bus at +39 3273564972 or via email <u>at</u>

info@thewinebus.net, and their office address is Contrada Bosco Lumeti 30, Montemiletto, 83038, Italy.

*Wine Tour in Tuscany* is a tour operator that offers a variety of wine tours, cooking classes and sightseeing tours in Tuscany specifically, including private tours and more customised ones. Owner Donnatella and her son Dario take you into the lesser-known or crowded parts of the Tuscan wine country, which very few people get to see. She prides herself on her wine knowledge, energy, creativity and passion. Both mother and son were born and raised in Siena and know Tuscany inside out. *(Wine Tour in Tuscany, 2022)* Tours have received positive reviews from customers who appreciate their very personalised service, knowledgeable guides and a good selection of wineries. Some customers noted that the tours can be expensive, but in general, this is true of Tuscany and that the quality of the experience justifies the cost. Getting what you pay for comes to mind, and in general, I have heard very good things. Wine Tour in Tuscany is a Tour Operator operating from Via F. di Valdambrino 5, 53100 Siena P.I. 01239320524 and more information is available on the website.

Now, *Italia Dolce Vita* is a unique travel experience company that I doubt would even want to fit into the 'tour operator' bracket as it specialises in luxury wine tours throughout Italy and is completely tailor-made as their unique selling proposition. They understand that whether your trip to Italy is a trip of a lifetime or you are returning to discover a new gem every year, you want everything to be perfect.

But of course, tailor-made trips come at a cost, and since they are designed exclusively for you, these trips need a budget to match. If this is your holiday bracket, then you can personalise everything from cultural, winery, and active experiences and mix in all the food and wine stops you like. *(Italia Dolce Vita, 2018)*

These experts in the world of bespoke travel will create your dream trip based on your needs, interests and budget and offer 24/7 support and assistance while travelling. *(Italia Dolce Vita, 2018)* They have received positive reviews from customers who praise ultra-high-end accommodations, excellent wine selections and knowledgeable guides. *Italia Dolce Vita* is contactable through the online enquiry form and by phone at (941) 960-7011.

Another few good wine tour companies include 'Grape Tours in Florence', offering premium wine tours from Florence for small groups of a maximum of 8 people and guided by local wine professionals and TOURSCANY, doing similar, at di Corrado Di Pompeo Via Consorti, 17 – 53010 Siena and contactable on +39 333 7019983 or email info@tourscany.it

Overall, all three of these options in the Italian wine scene have received positive reviews from customers and friends and are reputable options of different sizes for organising tours and tastings.

Moving on to the alternative - booking directly with a winery in Italy - can be a great option for those who want to have a personal and authentic experience, knowing there is no third-party involvement. When booking directly with a winery, you can often have a more personalised experience ultimately, without paying for the privilege, and can organise it directly with a member of staff or even a member of the winemaking family. You may have the opportunity to meet the winemakers and are more likely to learn about the winemaking process firsthand (refer to the joys of this listed in Chapter 1).

Additionally, the winery may be able to tailor the experience to your preferences, and there is more scope to give them an informal briefing on your group's preferences, size and how you would like the itinerary to run.

Booking directly with a winery can often be less expensive than booking through a tour operator or travel agency. This is because you're cutting out the middleman and dealing directly with the winery - no different to cutting out a hotel booking website, for example. It will also likely give you more flexibility in terms of scheduling and itinerary. The winery may be able to accommodate your schedule and preferences more easily than a tour operator or travel agency with set times and days - and they are far more likely to accommodate that one friend who can only eat lettuce or is gluten-free; bless them.

Another cool perk of booking directly with a winery is that you might get access to limited-production wines unavailable to the general public. Most wineries will give you access to these exclusive wines on a friendly direct tour, which always makes me feel I am getting something extra special from the experience. If you like to feel the same, then this may be for you. Needless to say, you are always supporting a local business too and contributing to the local economy by going direct - that never fails to be a good option when possible.

Going straight to the source can provide a personalised and authentic experience while potentially saving you money - but it's for those of us who have the time and secretly love being the group admin and can take charge of the itinerary.

If you have a specific winery in mind or are interested in a particular region or grape variety, booking directly with the winery can be a great option, meaning you skip out those parts you aren't as fussed about.

Whether you book directly with wineries or through a tour operator, it's important to research and read reviews before booking to ensure you're getting a quality experience at a fair price. The cost of a wine tour in Italy will also vary depending on the region, time of year, and level of luxury you want. For example, the hot air balloon arrival will cost whether you book directly or via an operator!

## What Do I Need to Pack?

Going on an Italian wine tour with a group of friends or your beloved partner (probably the former, ideally, right?) will be an exciting and memorable experience. If this can help plan with some tips on what to pack, how to deal with jetlag and some airport hacks to save even a few annoying mishaps, then mission accomplished!

When packing for an Italian wine tour, it's important to consider the weather and activities you'll be doing - so despite dreaming of looking like you're straight off the Milan catwalk ladies, it is rarely practical.

Can you still indulge in a new wide-brimmed hat and some new Breton stripes? Of course, you can. Italy can be warm in the summer months as mentioned, so pack lightweight clothing and comfortable shoes as a must - and comfort doesn't have to be ugly, I promise. You may also want sunscreen for vineyard tours, but good wineries are also likely to have sunscreen available for visitors' use. Additionally, you may want to pack a few dressier outfits for fine dining experiences and evening meals.

THE ITALIAN WINE TOUR POCKET GUIDE

*Figure 28. What to Pack*

Now, dealing with jetlag can be challenging at the best times, especially if you're travelling from a different time zone - add drinking wine during the day to this mix, and I get it...tiredness might get the better of you sometimes.

To minimise the effects of it, try to adjust your sleep schedule a few days before your trip and get into the swing of your 'new nighttime.' Additionally, try to stay hydrated during your flight and on arrival, and consider taking a nap when you arrive at your destination before the lunchtime wine-tasting - I can't promote naps highly enough as a qualified napper - for those of you who need help falling asleep, consider using earplugs and/or an eye mask or one of the many amazing podcasts available online or on Spotify.

Airport life hacks follow the same rules as travelling for any trip these days - leave as long as you possibly can to get to the airport to make your experience more pleasant and as stress-free as it can be from the outset. Also, check in online before you arrive at the airport to save time, and if you are the designated admin in charge of a larger wine trip group, then make sure everyone else is doing the same.

Bring an empty water bottle that you can fill up after security to avoid paying for bottled water. Otherwise, that hydration-on-travel I mentioned above can become expensive. The same applies to food - pack healthy snacks to avoid buying expensive and normally very average airport food.

I am not going to be like anyone's mum and say also wear comfortable clothes and slip-on shoes to make going through security easier and a more comfortable flight experience, but I somewhat am, and I would recommend it.

Overall, by packing appropriately, preparing for the inevitable jet-lag, and some simple airport hacks, you can make your Italian wine tour experience more enjoyable and stress-free from the start.

Now, just pray for no flight delays, and you're on your way!

*Figure 29. Map of Italy's Rail System*

## On arrival at the main airports

Getting to your chosen wine region(s) from the main airports in Italy can vary depending on your destination and mode of transportation - and, as mentioned above, whether you're choosing to have a local Italian hero in the form of a tour operator chauffeur to collect your party.

If not, and choosing the road less travelled approach, there are some general guidelines for getting to wine country from the main Italian airports:

- Roma (Fiumicino) Airport: From Roma airport (let's get into the swing of calling the eternal city by its Italian name, shall we? I already feel a holiday vibe coming on..), you can take a train or rent a car to get to the nearby wine regions such as Frascati, Castelli Romani or Umbria, which we cover again later in the book.

If you prefer taking the train, take the Leonardo Express train from the airport to Termini Station, then transfer to the regional trains serving all wine regions. If you'd rather have the freedom to rent your own car, many car rental agencies are available at the airport.

Many of the reliable car rental companies in Europe include Hertz and Europcar - both with a strong presence in all major cities and airports; Avis, which includes luxury vehicles and hybrid cars; and

Budget - a budget-friendly car rental company that offers competitive rates and smaller vehicle options.

The norm will apply that you should review the rental agreement and insurance coverage with any car rental company to avoid any surprises or additional costs, and then aim to survive the queue and get out of the airport as quickly as possible!

- Milan (Malpensa) Airport: From here, if you can resist stopping by the shops (not possible in my case), you can take a train from Milano - or, of course, rent a car to get to the nearby wine regions, which include Franciacorta or the famous Piemonte. If the train works well for you and a car isn't an option, then the train line you are looking for is the Malpensa Express train from the airport to Milan Central Station, where it is worth noting I have locked my luggage for a few hours in a locker in the downstairs facility to merrily explore the city for a few hours minus the suitcases.

From there, you transfer to the regional trains serving the wine regions, and it is a large and self-explanatory, well-signposted train station out to the Lakes and beyond. Again, if you prefer to rent a car, many of the same European normal car rental agencies are available at the airport.

- Tuscany (Florence) Airport: From Florence airport, you can take a bus (hello, new mode of transport option!) or rent a car to get to the nearby wine regions such as Chianti and Montepulciano. If you like taking the bus and are not in a hurry, it's certainly the most cost-effective option and easy enough. Take the Volainbus bus from the airport to the Florence Santa Maria Novella train station, then transfer to the local buses that connect all the major wine regions.

- Sicily (Palermo) Airport: From Palermo airport, your main options are more car-centric on the islands, and you can basically only rent a car or take a taxi to get to the nearby wine regions such as Marsala or Alcamo. If you prefer taking a taxi and don't fancy combining driving with wine tasting, then that's fair enough and probably a good shout - you can find a taxi rank outside the arrivals terminal and just be prepared to include this in the overall costs for the trip.

If your planned wine tour is to the main airports covered above - Rome, Milan, Florence or Palermo - there are a few basic train systems briefly touched on above that are helpful to know more about on arrival to help you reach wine territory. Sorry if you are heading to another; it's hard to cover the whole rail system of Italy, but I hope this helps many of you! Here are some of the main train systems in Italy that can take you to wine regions:

*Trenitalia* is the national train company in Italy and offers high-speed and regional trains throughout the country. Many wine regions can be reached via Trenitalia, including Tuscany, Umbria and Sicily. From Rome, for example, you can take a high-speed train to Florence or a regional train to Orvieto, which is located in the Umbria wine region and is central to reaching many of the Umbria winery boltholes on your list.

*Italo* is a private, ultra-high-speed train company that also operates across Italy. It offers service between major cities such as Rome, Florence and Milan and can be a good option for reaching wine regions quickly at opposite ends of the country or larger distances. If landing in Florence, (1. Very lucky, and 2...) you take an Italo train to the Chianti wine region, located just south of the city.

There are many smaller regional train lines from many of the other airports, but the above are the main train systems you need to know to reach many wine regions in Italy from the primary airports, while Ferrovie del Sud Est is another good option for reaching the wine regions exclusively in southern parts of Italy. I suggest you check schedules and book tickets in advance, using your best Italian or making friends with someone local to ensure all goes to plan on arrival.

If you haven't opted for the transport-included tour operator packages, renting a car offers the most flexibility to access the vineyards and choose when to come and go. But needless to say, to ditch trains entirely and go for a hire car, someone has to be responsible and not be over the drink/ drive limit on the group's behalf, but you can always take turns so often it isn't a problem.

If you have gone it alone and are self-planning your wine excursions, then public transportation can be a good option if you don't feel comfortable driving on the other side of the road (English travellers - heads up) or want to avoid the hassle of parking, etc.

Remember that some wineries require advance reservations, so it's best to plan to ensure whichever options you choose, you have a smooth trip there and start on a high note.

## Basic Italian Wine Language Phrases and Pronunciation

As if we weren't already too good to you, I will offer my basic Italian lingo for your enjoyment and use on a wine tour. Think of it as a very limited and wine-focused Italian dictionary that should never be shared with an actual Italian-speaking friend to save my shame. When heading to Italian wine territory for la dolce vita, knowing some basic Italian phrases can help communicate either with locals to find your way or the doubtless-completely-charming winemakers. It also means getting the most out of your experience and pushing yourself to fit in with local culture. Here are some basic Italian phrases and pronunciation tips in phonetics to get you started!

Hello - Ciao (chow)

Goodbye - Arrivederci (a-ree-veh-dehr-chee)

Please - Per favore (pehr fah-voh-reh)

Thank you - Grazie (grah-tsee-eh)

You're welcome - Prego (preh-goh)

Excuse me - Scusi (skoo-zee) *this has to be a favourite*

Do you speak English? - Parla inglese? (pahr-lah een-gleh-zeh?) *Ideally if you have learned nothing else, practise this one!*

I don't understand - Non capisco (nohn kah-pee-skoh)

Can you help me? - Mi può aiutare? (mee pwoh ah-yoo-tah-reh?)

Where is the winery? - Dov'è la cantina? (doh-veh lah kahn-tee-nah?) *Essential*

Additionally, here are some wine-specific terms that may come in handy during your tour - hoping by this point you've found your way there:

Wine - Vino (vee-noh)

Red wine - Vino rosso (vee-noh roh-soh)

White wine - Vino bianco (vee-noh bee-ahn-koh)

Wine tasting - Degustazione di vino (deh-goo-stah-tsee-oh-neh dee vee-noh)

Vineyard - Vigneto (veen-yeh-toh)

Winery - Cantina (kahn-tee-nah)

Bottle - Bottiglia (boh-tee-lyah)

Glass - Bicchiere (bee-kyeh-reh)

Remember that pronunciation is key in Italian (even more so than an overemphasised hand gesture), so make sure to drop the self-consciousness and just go for it with a true *Italiano* accent. You may also want to bring a phrasebook or use a translation app to help with communication if it goes less according to plan or you forget all these phrases on day one.

## Useful Contacts and Emergency Numbers

Now, there is absolutely no reason to think anything is more likely to go wrong on your Italian trip than in any other country or our everyday lives. But that said, it is a good idea to familiarise yourself with the few important emergency numbers in Italy if planning, *just in case of an emergency*, and to have these at the ready.

Like all of Europe, Italy has one number to call in case of an emergency, which is 112. This is the best number to call for foreign nationals visiting for holidays, as calls are also answered in English, French and German as needed. The above few phrases in Italian won't get you that far; I'm afraid of the serious stuff.

Italy also has three other emergency numbers for specific purposes, namely the following:

- 113 for Police assistance

- 115 for the Fire Brigade

- 118 for First Aid

*(Italy Now, 2020)*

*Figure 30. Italian Police Car*

Print out these numbers if helpful; otherwise, Google can tell you the same instantly. Similarly, it is also a good idea to note the phone number of your country's embassy in Italy. This is trickier to get hold of sometimes and should be your go-to contact for any less imminent danger but serious emergency requiring consulate assistance. Here are some phone numbers of the embassies/consulates of specific popular tourist countries visiting Italy:

**United States of America**

Rome Embassy – 06-46-741

Milan Consulate – 02-290-351

Florence Consulate – 055-266-951

Naples Consulate – 081-583-8111

**United Kingdom**

Rome Embassy – 06-4220-0001

Milan Consulate – 02-732-001

**Australia**

Rome Embassy – 06-8527-21

Milan Consulate – 02-7767-4200

**Germany**

Rome Embassy – 06-49-2131

Milan Consulate – 02-623-1101

*(Italy Now, 2020)*

If you are in Italy when any disaster strikes, you can still use many of the same techniques and practises you already know if an emergency happens at home. I have high hopes we don't need to apply any of these things above, but they are there for your reference if needed. Learning how to apply first aid in any environment is also a tremendous skill to learn - it is on my list this year, and I have no excuse.

## Summary of Chapter 3

In summary, I hope this chapter has given you an unbiased and helpful breakdown of some of the administrative (yawn) and practical things to remember when planning and enjoying a wine holiday in Italy.

On reflection, a good time to visit Italy for a wine tour holiday is typically during the shoulder seasons of Spring (i.e. April to June) and Autumn harvest time (September to November) when the weather is mild, and the crowds are less overbearing. But that is down to preference - if you like baking, then summer can be hot and sometimes more crowded, but certainly a buzzy vibe; just go prepared. Winter can be cold and rainy, though many regions like Tuscany are still lovely in the winter, so pack a raincoat, and you'll still have a cracking time.

We covered some of the most famous regions, including Tuscany and Piemonte, and how these tend to mean more expensive price points in wine tastings, accommodation, and additional costs on the trip. By contrast, Puglia, Umbria, and Sicily can offer more cost-effective versions of a winery experience, still offering high-quality wines and a seriously good holiday.

Regarding the general cost of travel, I hope I have been transparent in saying Italy can be expensive, particularly in the major cities and tourist hotspots. My advice is to either budget for that and embrace it if you're happy to do so or not fall into the traps of the flagship wine regions and travel options to get there otherwise. Either way, make sure to budget accordingly and get the money belt at ready for safety -is it even a holiday without one? Plan for any additional expenses like meals, transportation and wine purchases sent home by the caseload and enjoy every second.

Finally, as if I could be impartial about how beautiful Italy was and how many must-see cities and attractions there are along the way, this chapter covered an overview of transportation and language options to help you from most major Italian airports and how to reach wine country from them.

If you have the luxury of a day or two stopover in these cities before or after the tour, please jump at the chance! Attractions in Italy include the Colosseum and Vatican City in Rome, the Duomo and Uffizi Gallery in Florence, and the canals and Piazza San Marco in Venice.

For wine lovers, it will also be a chance to see the local region's wines on the buzzing tables of cute tavernas and restaurants and to sample the wines in real-time with local cuisine.

Overall, your wine tour holiday will be an unforgettable experience. Make sure to plan, research the regions you want to visit, budget accordingly and have the time of your life - just jot down a few Italian phrases in the meantime!

CHAPTER 4

# TOUR OF NORTHERN ITALY'S WINE REGIONS

Northern Italy is home to some of the most renowned wine regions in the country, including Piemonte, Lombardy and Veneto - some of these being the famed 'flagship' national wine regions shared previously. Each region has its own distinctive characteristics and specialities, reflecting the climate, soil and winemaking traditions of the area. In this chapter, we will take a closer look at these regions in the North of the country, highlighting the best wineries to visit, what is on offer there, and some of the best wines produced.

*Figure 31. Piemonte*

## Piemonte

Piemonte, (or Piedmont in English spelling and seen very often) is located in the North-West corner of Italy, spreading over 9,700 mi$^2$ (25.300 sq km) from the Alps to the Mediterranean with a population of more than 4,300,000 inhabitants. *(Meet Piemonte tours, 2022)* It borders France in the West, Switzerland in the North, and Lombardy in the East - the region we will explore next. The southern side is met by the Apennines mountains, which divide the region from the Liguria region (Meet Piemonte tours, 2022), and the sparkling Mediterranean coast is, therefore, only ever a short drive away, my friends.

The vicinity to Milan, the French Riviera, Portofino and Lake Como make the Piemonte region of Italy, not only beyond trendy and the holiday hotspot people flock to from the world over but accessible in the sense you can get to it from all directions through a well- connected network of highways and railroads. *(Meet Piemonte tours, 2022)* Piemonte is easily accessible through the Turin airport and the nearby Milan Malpensa and Genoa airports.

Piemonte is the second largest Italian region after Sicily and is known for its red wines - some of which we shared in our introduction, notably Barolo and Barbaresco. These wines are made from the Nebbiolo grape variety and are well known worldwide as go-to wine labels, with a rich, complex character and notes of dark fruit, spices and tobacco.

The region's wine production is concentrated in the Langhe hills, where the hilly terrain and cool climate provide the ideal conditions for the Nebbiolo grape. The mix of soils, microclimates and altitudes make it perfect for the most epic grapevines. The microclimates vary depending on the altitude and proximity to the Tanaro River, which provides natural irrigation for the vineyards. But the Protected Designation of Origin (PDO) makes the Barolo and Barbaresco wines such high-quality: A PDO status protects them and must adhere to strict regulations to ensure quality and authenticity. This includes limiting the grape yields per hectare, ageing the wines for at least two years, and using only specific grape varieties and winemaking techniques.

*Figure 32. A Bottle of Barolo Wine*

So, where do you try these famous red wines, Barolo and Barbaresco? In general, geographically, the area set at the foot of the Alps, just west of Lake Maggiore and Milan Malpensa airport, is known for the cultivation of Nebbiolo grapes producing these wines. Regarding the differences between the two, the Barolo area has medium temperatures due to its proximity to the Alps and the warm winds rising from the Tanaro valley, whereas the area around

Barbaresco is more uniform, has warmer temperatures, and has less rainfall. (www.langevini.it, 2022)

So you don't need to venture far once you set foot on Italian soil from Milan airport for many excellent wineries - what a bonus. I am sharing some of the best wineries I know well, including a selection of both large and small operations to try the famous Barolo and Barbaresco, as well as luxury to cost-effective options:

- Marchesi di Barolo: Marchesi di Barolo is one of the oldest and most prestigious wineries in Barolo and one I promised we would come back to! They offer guided tours and tastings and also have a gorgeous restaurant on-site. Commendatore Pietro Abbona, the winery founder from the early 1900s is considered the real patriarch of Barolo, who first produced the wine from his land in the estate of Marchesa Falletti. *(www.marchesibarolo.com, 2023)* The family still runs the estate today - Ernesto and Anna with their children Valentina and Davide, who have ensured winemaking has stayed in the family for six generations.

*Figure 33. Marchesi di Barolo*

Wines range in price with some impressive riserva bottles for sale and normal varietals, and they offer a wide selection of Barolo and other signature Piemonte wines. The historic cellars on site are open for you to visit as well, and you can find the estate at Via Roma, 1, 12060 Barolo (CN) or phone +39 0173 564419 and email reception@marchesibarolo.com for any visit enquiries. Open every day from 10.30 to 18.00

- Gaja Winery: Gaja is another of the most well-known wineries in Piemonte, possibly Italy, and is known for its high-end Barbaresco wines. In the district of Langhe we covered above, this is a big-name winery you will recognise the name of in your own local supermarkets, I'm sure. It chiefly produces several Barbaresco and Barolo wines and later diversified into Brunello di Montalcino and "Super Tuscan" wine production.

Its current owner and president, Angelo Gaja, is credited with developing techniques that have revolutionised winemaking in Italy, and he is coined "the king of Barbaresco" as if we needed a king for every wine, right? Angelo and his daughter Gaia are central to the warmth and ease of their family-run business *(Wine Spectator, 2022)* as they willingly recount stories behind Gaja's Tuscan wines, Ca'Marcanda and Pieve Santa Restituta Sugarille. *(Wine Spectator, 2022)*

*Figure 34. A Bottle of Barbaresco Wine*

It is certainly true that Barbaresco wine is considered a status symbol, and Gaja now exports its version of the wine globally to huge success. The current Gaja estate owns 240 acres of vineyards in the Barbaresco DOCG (Barbaresco and Treiso) and the Barolo DOCG (Serralunga d'Alba and La Morra) *(Wilson Daniels, 2023)*. The winery is exclusive and retains some of its exclusivity by offering only high-end, bespoke tours, tastings and appointments, which are certainly required. Some wine tour companies can arrange visits here, but essentially, as of 2023, those interested in visiting Gaja winery are invited to donate a minimum of €300 per person to a specially chosen charity. In exchange, Gaja offers a personalised tour of vineyards and cellars and a tasting of some of the best Nebbiolo varietals in Italy. *(All Wine Tours, 2023)* The winery is also home to a Michelin-starred restaurant, making it an ideal destination for a high-end wine trip and one of the experiences for true wine and food lovers.

- Produttori del Barbaresco: Produttori del Barbaresco is a cooperative winery that local growers own, and you really feel a sense of supporting a community here. It is the opposite of the above-mentioned Gaja but its charm and quality are equally paramount. They offer affordable tours and tastings and are known for producing exclusively Barbaresco wines and doing exactly what it says on the tin. Their company structure means that the winery can offer good quality wines at a more affordable price point, and their tagline is simply brilliant: "One grape, Nebbiolo. One wine, Barbaresco." There is no mixed messaging here, folks. You can find Produttori del Barbaresco in the heart of the Barbaresco DOCG appellation at Via Torino, 54 12050 Barbaresco CN, I or by phone. +39 0173635139 to arrange a visit. More information online at www.produttoridelbarbaresco.com

- Azelia Winery: Azelia Winery is a family-owned winery in Barolo that offers tours and tastings by appointment. The family-owned aspect is felt in every inch of it, and they produce a range of Barolo wines, including some single-vineyard selections. The family farm is 16 hectares with an average production of 85,000 bottles per year. Luigi is at the helm, supported by his wife Lorella and son Lorenzo, who represent the fifth generation of wine producers. (www.azelia.it, 2022) The winery has a really friendly and welcoming atmosphere and is a good option for those looking for a smaller, more intimate winery experience where you leave knowing everyone's names and booking your return trip. Bookings for wine tours are by appointment only by phone at +39 0173 62859 or via email at l.scavino@azelia.it. The address is Via Alba Barolo 143, 12060 Castiglione Falletto (CN)

- Fontanafredda Winery: By contrast, yet again, Fontanafredda Winery is one of the largest wineries in Piemonte and another one of the most well-known in Italy. Founded by the first King of Italy, no less, yes you read that correctly, it is a piece of the love story between King Vittorio Emanuele II, and Rosa Vercellana. (www.fontanafredda.it, 2023) Today, this impressive icon of a wine estate is over 120 hectares of organic crops that frame Italy's early fairytales.

Fontanafredda is also currently the largest private producer of Barolo, including Barolo Serralunga d'Alba and Barolo Classico, and their production accounts for around 6% of the entire appellation. Partly thanks to its impressive size and scope for organic practice and education, Fontanafredda offers a variety of tours and tastings on a larger and more commercial scale, including an underground tour of its cellars. The wide range of wines could take you all day to try, and they have a large and impressive restaurant on-site for lunch. You can contact them by phone at +39 0173 626 111 or email at info@fontanafredda.it - or choose from a selection of visit types on the website at www.villaggionarrante.it/cantine/visite-in-cantina/

*Figure 35. Map of Barolo and Barbaresco Regions*

These wineries are a must-do for anyone visiting the region for its signature wines. All of the above offer various experiences and price points, from cost-effective to luxury and Michelin-starred food pairings. All will be producing high-quality Barolo and Barbaresco wines, which are excellent options for those looking to explore the famous grape varieties of Piemonte, depending on your group's preference and budget.

Most of the wineries in the region are easily accessible by car, taxi or public transportation from cities like Turin, Asti or Alba. It is worth noting that different types of wine are bottled in Northern Piemonte, including those found above, so venture further to the top of Piemonte to find Gattinara, Ghemme, Colli Novaresi, and more. *(Meet Piemonte tours, 2022)* Meanwhile, the countryside north of Turin is the area to head to specifically for producing Canavese wines and Erbaluce. *(Meet Piemonte tours, 2022)* Moving to the wineries offering these other varietals elsewhere in Piemonte, the region is home to many other excellent wineries exploring different grape varieties and in the path less travelled by wine folk - Here are some of the best and how to get to them:

- Contratto Winery: Contratto Winery is located in the town of Canelli, in the Asti region of Piemonte. It is known for producing high-quality sparkling wines, including a rare and highly sought-after Metodo Classico

Contratto For England. To get to Contratto Winery, you can rent a car or take a taxi from nearby cities like Asti or Alba - this isn't one to try out public transport to get to!

- Ceretto Winery: Ceretto Winery covers four winery estates located in the town of Alba and is known for producing the classic Barolo and Barbaresco wines as well, but also Arneis, a brilliant white wine from the Roero region.

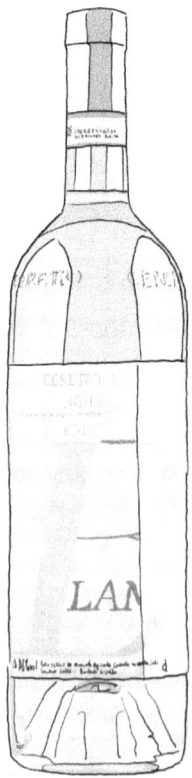

*Figure 36. Langhe DOC Arneis Blange*

They offer tours and tastings on-site at each of their four impressive wineries, including one in a wine-tasting tower in the vineyards. To get there, you can either walk or take a taxi from the centre of Alba for some of these. Thirty-five years ago, the Ceretto family found an old farmstead on Alba's outskirts, now its main office. This estate, known as Monsordo Bernardina, is the company's main hub and home to the production of the wine labels. ( 2023)

More than 30 hectares of vineyards, both traditional and international varieties, are on-site surrounding the farmstead, and all are grown sustainably. Expect high-end dining here, though - together with chef Enrico Crippa, this is home to the Piazza Duomo restaurant, the only three Michelin-starred restaurant in the region. The four estates comprising Ceretto are Monsordo Bernardina Estate, Bricco Rocche Winery, Bricco Asili Winery and I Vignaioli di Santo Stefano. Contact Ceretto by phone at +39 0173 282582 or at  To organise a wine tour or visit, phone +39 0173 268033 or email visit@ceretto.com

- Pio Cesare Winery: Pio Cesare Winery is also located in the heart of the town of Alba. The cellars are some of the few still operating in the historical centre and were built at the end of the 1700s. These cellars are situated on four different ground levels, some so deep that you are underneath the Tanaro River. It is like stepping back in time here and a great chance to see the fermentation and ageing of the wines in oak casks, then barrels and in bottles first-hand. They offer tours and tastings by appointment and are easily accessible for anyone on foot for the day in Alba Centre. Tours are available from Monday to Saturday morning. Please call them at +39 (0)173 440386 or email visits@piocesare.it to pre-book.

The winery is closed on Sunday all day and on public or national holidays.

Equally, there are many other great winery options near or around Turin if you come from there. The following is accessible from the city, which is a major transportation hub in the region and might be a helpful base if you are looking to do several winery day trips from one central base during your trip:

- La Spinetta Winery: La Spinetta Winery is located in Castagnole Lanze, about a 60-minute drive from Turin. They produce a range of high-quality wines, including the famed Piemonte names of Barbaresco and Moscato d'Asti, and offer tours and tastings by appointment. You can contact them at Via Annunziata, 17. 14054 - Castagnole delle Lanze (At) Phone number: +39 0141 877 396 / +39 335 1389 359 Email: info@la-spinetta.com Website: https://www.la-spinetta.com/en/winery/la-spinetta/

- Cascina degli Ulivi Winery: Cascina degli Ulivi Winery is located in the town of Moncucco Torinese, about a 30-minute drive from Turin. This biodynamic winery produces wines made from indigenous grape varieties like Grignolino and Freisa. They also have an on-site restaurant that serves traditional Piedmontese cuisine. You can book through their website: https://www.cascinadegliulivi.it/?lang=en. Address: Strada della Mazzola, 12 15067 Novi Ligure. Phone number: +39 0143/744598. To book visits and wine tastings, contact Luigi at vino@cascinadegliulivi.it

- Tenuta Roletto Winery: Tenuta Roletto Winery is located in the town of Cuceglio - which is about a 50-minute drive from Turin. It is an organic winery that produces a range of wines, including whites made from the Erbaluce grape, native to the region. They offer tours and by appointment and also have a restaurant on-site that serves local dishes. Contact them at https://www.tenutaroletto.it/. The address is Via Porta Pia, 69, 10090 Cuceglio TO. Phone Number: +39 0124 492293

These wineries offer visitors unique experiences and are easily accessible from Turin by car or public transportation. You are likely to get a real taste of Piemonte's charm and culture, and many are known for their commitment to sustainable and organic winemaking practices and age-old wine techniques.

Lastly, the foot of the western Alps near the town of Saluzzo has its own grape cultivation and wine production that is charming to see and the least-known area in the Piemonte region to make a beeline for. You can find a range of family-run and specialised wineries in this area, which are all proud to show you their vineyards and bottlings.

- Cascina Disa Winery: Cascina Disa is a family-run winery in the town of Manta, just outside Saluzzo. They produce a range of wines, including Dolcetto, Barbera and Nebbiolo - all of which are made from grapes grown on-site at their estate. They offer tours and tastings by appointment only.  Get in touch through their website: http://www.cascinadisa.com/ Address: Azienda agriviticola Elio Sandri. Località Perno 14 12065 Monforte d'Alba. Email: info@cascinadisa.com

- Azienda Agricola Gian Piero Marrone Winery: Azienda Agricola Gian Piero Marrone is located in the town of La Morra, about a 45-minute drive from Saluzzo. They produce an array of wines, including Barolo, Dolcetto, and Barbera, all of which are made from grapes grown on their estate. They also offer tours and tastings only by appointment. Contact them at: https://www.agricolamarrone.com/ Address: Via Annunziata, 13, 12064 La Morra Phone Number: +39 0173 509288

These wineries offer unique experiences for visitors and are known for their commitment to producing high-quality wines from their own grape cultivation.

If you want to experience a selection of the wineries in Piemonte and have time for a longer holiday, then a Piemonte Wine Tour Vacation, packaged by *Meet Piemonte Tours*, is a 6-day holiday in the region which encompasses many of the above and the region's best grape varieties, taking in all of northwest Italy's charm and its renowned wine scene in a divinely well-organised itinerary. A 5-night stay in wine resorts and boutique hotels surrounded by vineyards makes for a happy holiday, I can assure you. This is a great option for those who don't want the planning and have at least a few days to play with in one area. You will take in all of the vineyards of northern Piedmont and Gavi, onwards to Colline Novaresi, Alba, Asti, Barolo, Barbaresco and Nizza Monferrato. Bellissimo indeed. *(Meet Piemonte Tours, 2022)* Find the team at their office on Via Cordara 34, 14049, Nizza Monferrato (AT) and contact them by phone at +39 344 111 4522 or email info@meetpiemonte.com to book. Office hours: Monday – Friday 9 am-5 pm.

However you choose to see the Piemonte region, it won't disappoint. Heading South slightly from Piemonte, join us across the regional border in Lombardy - our next stop in the regional tour of Northern Italy.

## Lombardy

Lombardy, located next to Piemonte in Northern Italy, is known for producing a variety of high-quality wines but is perhaps best known for its sparkling wines made in the Franciacorta region using the "traditional method." It is made similarly to Champagne, and these wines are known for their crisp and elegant character.

*Figure 37. Lombardy*

Also known as the "méthode champenoise," the traditional method used in Lombardy involves a secondary fermentation in the bottle, creating the carbonation characteristic of sparkling wines. I can hear a cork popping already somewhere. The basic steps involved in making sparkling wines, which you might be lucky enough to see in some wineries in the region, include the following:

- Primary fermentation: The first step is to ferment the base wine in stainless steel tanks, oak barrels, or both. The wine uses Chardonnay, Pinot Noir, and/or Pinot Blanc grapes and is typically dry with high acidity.

- Blending: After the primary fermentation is complete, the winemaker will blend different wines to achieve the desired style and flavour for the final sparkling wine.

- Secondary fermentation: The blended wine is then bottled with the addition of yeast and sugar, which triggers a second fermentation in the bottle. The wine is aged on its lees (i.e. the dead yeast cells) for a period of time, which adds complexity and richness to the wine.

- Riddling: After the wine has been aged on its lees (see above, not a typo) for the desired amount of time, the bottles are gradually turned and tilted to move the lees towards the neck of the bottle.

- Disgorging: The neck of the bottle is then frozen, and the frozen lees are removed by quickly opening the bottle and allowing the pressure to expel the frozen sediment.

- Dosage: A small amount of sugar is added to the wine to balance the acidity and add sweetness if desired.

- Ageing: The final step is to age the wine for a period of time before it is released, allowing the flavours and aromas to integrate and develop further.

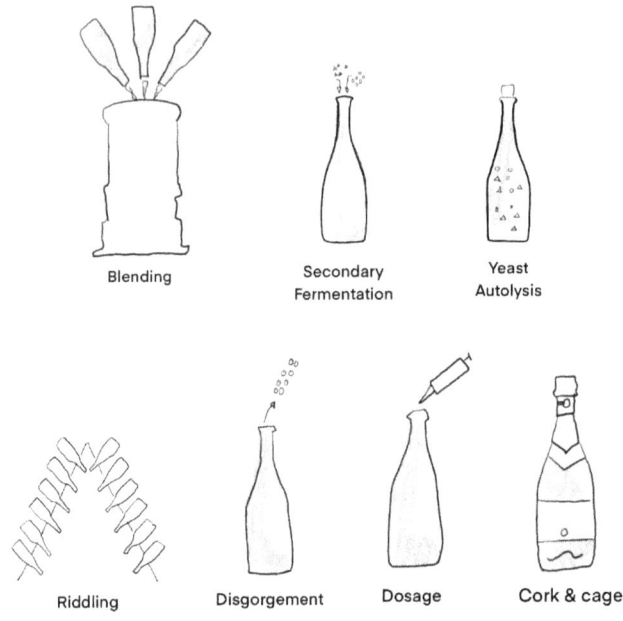

*Figure 38. Méthode Champenoise*

As mentioned, the main grape varieties used in producing Franciacorta wines are Chardonnay, Pinot Noir, and/or Pinot Blanc. Therefore, These are the signature grape varieties you see growing in the Lombardy region, producing quality sparkling varietals. The result is a fizzy, wonderful, typically dry wine with a fairly high acidity.

Prosecco and Franciacorta are both prides of Northern Italy: Prosecco is produced in the regions of Veneto we get to next, and Friuli-Venezia Giulia (North-East) while Franciacorta is produced and can only be produced in this province in the Lombardy region. *(Lake Como for you, 2022)*

A few recommended wineries to see these wines and some stages of the aforementioned process include the following:

- Ca' del Bosco Winery: Ca' del Bosco is located in the Franciacorta region and offers guided tours of their vineyards and cellars and tastings of their Franciacorta wines. Here, the winery has been acknowledged for certified organic viticulture (more simply the cultivation or culture of grapes) which means the grapevine cultivation is a more mindful approach, focused on maintaining a balance between the multiple ecosystems and protecting the land. The experience would include learning about the traditional method of sparkling wine production from start to finish, as well as the history and terroir of the area and what makes the wines organic. Website: https://www.cadelbosco.com/en/

- Bellavista Winery: Bellavista is also located in the Franciacorta region of Lombardy and is known for producing high-quality sparkling wines. The winery offers a similar experience to the above, but I would like to spend some extra time on this special winery, founded in the early 1970s and has since become known for producing some of the finest sparkling wines in Italy. Website: https:/

/franciacorta.wine/en/wineries/bellavista/ Address: Via Bellavista, 4 Phone Number: +39 0307762000 Email: info@bellavistawine.it

For those of you whose ears pricked up in Chapter 2 about seeing the whole process of winemaking first-hand, this is the place for you. The Bellavista Winery offers guided tours of their vineyards and cellars and a behind-the-scenes look at the traditional process. The tours typically last around two hours and are led by knowledgeable guides who can answer any questions you may have about the winery and its incredible wines.

The Winery Bellavista represents the excellence of Italian sparkling wine, near the Po Valley with 190 hectares of vineyards with the best exposure, cultivating grapes with viticulture that interprets nature - and results in cracking wines.

During a tour here, you will have the opportunity to explore the vineyards, where you will learn about the grape varieties grown at Bellavista and the unique terrain of the Franciacorta región.

The tour around the cellars includes visiting the bottling room to see how the wines are carefully bottled and corked. The tour concludes with a tasting of Bellavista's sparkling wines, which include Franciacorta Brut, Franciacorta Satèn and a sublime Franciacorta Rosé. The wines are paired with local cheeses and other delicacies as an added touch to the charm of your cheers moment among the vineyards.

*Figure 39. Bellavista Alma Brut*

A visit to Bellavista Winery is necessary for anyone interested in sparkling wines and the winemaking process. The guided tour of the vineyards and cellars provides a brilliant insight into the world of traditional winemaking, while their sparkling wines are pretty epic, too. From Bellavista comes about one million bottles of fine Italian wine every year, most of this being sparkling, but not forgetting the fine whites and reds if this is more of your taste and tasty brandy production.

In addition to sparkling wines made in the region, as with Bellavista many in Lombardy also produce high-quality red and white wines from various grape varieties. Some of the most important red grape varieties grown in Lombardy include Nebbiolo, Barbera, and Bonarda. The best winery to see these, in my opinion, is:

- Nino Negri Winery: Nino Negri is located in the Valtellina region of Lombardy, which is known for producing Nebbiolo wines. The winery offers tours and tastings of their Nebbiolo wines, as well as local specialities like Bresaola and Pizzoccheri. The experience would include learning about the unique terroir of the Valtellina region, as well as the history and winemaking techniques used to produce Nebbiolo wines. You can learn more about the winery and experiences here at https://www.ninonegri.it/en. Address: Via Ghibellini, 3, 23030 Chiuro, Sondrio. Phone Number: +39 0 342 485211 Email: n.negri@giv.it

The Valtellina region, located in the northern part of Lombardy near the Swiss border, is known for producing these red wines made from Nebbiolo grapes, which are known locally as Chiavennasca. These wines are often compared to Barolo and Barbaresco wines from the neighbouring Piemonte region we covered above and are also known for their elegance and complexity. The Valtellina area has some outstanding winery experiences as well, namely:

- The Mamete Prevostini Winery: Mamete Prevostini is a

relatively new winery in the Valtellina region, which has quickly gained a reputation for producing exceptional Nebbiolo wines and is part of the cool new wine scene there, offering great wine tastings with a decent hunk of local cheese along with it. Winning if you ask me. Contact them at : https://www.mameteprevostini.com/ Address: Via Don Primo Lucchinetti, 63, 23020 Mese, Sondrio. Phone number: +39 0343 41522  Email: degustazioni@mameteprevostini.com

- Rainoldi Winery: Rainoldi is a family-run winery that has been producing wines in this area since the early 20th century. They are known for their Nebbiolo wines, as well as their Sforzato di Valtellina, a sought-after wine made from dried Nebbiolo grapes. This is one for the social media posts aesthetically, and you'll leave with an incredible knowledge of their vineyards and cellars. Get in touch at: https://rainoldi.com/  Address: Via Stelvio, 128, 23030 Chiuro Sondrio.  Phone number: +39 0342 482225  Email: degustazionivinivaltellina.it

- Balgera Winery: Balgera is a small, family-run winery that has been producing wines here for over 400 years. They are known for similar wines to the above as well as the same dried grape speciality wine you won't find in many places. You will try a generous range of wines as well as their local speciality snacks. Info at: https://www.vinibalgera.it/contatti  Address: Corso Maurizio Quadrio, 26, 23030 Chiuro, Sondrio. Phone Number: +39 0342

482203   Email: info@vinibalgera.it

Finally, I can't give a huge shout-out to La Costa Winery in Lombardy, located in the Oltrepò Pavese area of the region and known for producing Barbera wines we tried in Piemonte. It is located in the village of Sona, and if you have a car for your Lombardy wine tour of dreams, then it is easily accessible from the A4 motorway. Take the exit for Sommacampagna and follow the signs for Sona. If you're travelling by public transportation, then yay for being able to try more wines. The easiest way to get there is by taking a train to the nearby city of Verona. From Verona, you can take a bus to the town of Sona and then a short taxi ride to the winery.

*Figure 40. Lombardy's regions*

Once you arrive at La Costa, it's all friendly staff, sunshine and wine - who can ask for more? You will be taken on a tour of the vineyards and cellars, learn about the winery's history, understand the unique terroir of the Valpolicella region, and see the winemaking process from grape to bottle. You'll also have the opportunity to taste some of the winery's best wines, including Valpolicella Classico, Ripasso and Amarone. All of them are brilliant, highly recommended examples of these wines synonymous with the area and region - and if you only have a chance to do one winery in Lombardy, I suggest you make it La Costa! Info at: Address: Agriturismo La Costa. Via Curone, 15. Phone Number: +390395312218 Email: info@la-costa.it

Now, onwards and across to Veneto, my wine-loving friends...

## Veneto

Veneto is located in Northeastern Italy and is known for its beautiful cities and stunning landscapes and as a world-class wine region. Its flagship city, Venice, is one of the most iconic cities in the world and is a must-see for anyone visiting Veneto. Nothing immerses you more in Italian culture than being on a gondola ride on the canals of Venice with an ice cream in your hand (just me?), passing landmarks like St. Mark's Basilica and the Doge's Palace.

The incredible city of water isn't the only city worth seeing in the region - Verona and other cities nearby also have a rich history and cultural heritage that are certainly worth visiting. If you are looking to flee the crowds, then you can explore the Dolomites mountain range located in the northern part of Veneto, which in winter boasts the famous ski resorts of Cortina d'Ampezzo or, in warmer months, offers hikes through the breathtaking landscapes. Veneto is also known for its famous lakes, such as Lake Garda, and its delicious cuisine, including risotto, polenta and world-famous seafood.

*Figure 41. Veneto*

In terms of wine, and what else are we here for?... the Veneto region is well-known for its red wines, particularly Amarone. Amarone is made using a traditional method where grapes are left to dry on straw mats for several months before being pressed.

Veneto also produces other high-quality, well-known wines, including our favourite bubbles, Prosecco. The Prosecco region is located in the hills north of Venice and is known for its sparkling wines. There are plenty of opportunities to take a wine tour of the region, visit local wineries and sample some of the best Prosecco wines in the world. Finally, this celebrated wine region is also known for its Valpolicella and Soave wines - basically, it does almost all varietals very well, and since Veneto is such an established wine region, you are likely to come across the obvious and largest wineries with ease:

- Bisol Winery: Bisol is one of the most well-known Prosecco producers in the Veneto region and one you would want to see and experience if you want to fo 'flagship' Veneto wineries. The winery is located in the Valdobbiadene area, about an hour's drive from Venice. To get there, you can rent a car or take a bus from Venice to Valdobbiadene, so it is doable however you are travelling. The vineyards are stylish rows of golden Glera grapes in a hilly landscape that is steeped in the tradition of making Prosecco Superiore. A tasting or tour here is full of passion and professionalism, and you can either do a tour and/or tasting of the Classics here or the Crus - all bookable at https://bisol.it/bisol/en/book-your-visit/ with at least 48 hours notice.

- Allegrini Winery: The Allegrini winery is a renowned Valpolicella producer located in the town of Fumane. Allegrini's estate extends for around 150 hectares in the cradle of the Valpolicella Classica. The vineyards yield prestigious wines stemming from the company's winemaking heritage and its proudly exclusively estate-grown grapes. It is about a 30-minute' drive from Verona, or you can take a train from Verona to the nearby town of Sant'Ambrogio and then a short taxi ride as well. Find out more at www.allegrini.it/

- Tommasi Winery: Tommasi is another well-known Valpolicella producer located in the town of Pedemonte, approximately the same distance away from Verona. It is part of a much bigger winemaking dynasty across Italy, and the Tommasi Family Estates has enjoyed decades of expansion to today when they own 600 hectares of land in some of Italy's most intriguing and prestigious winemaking regions. To get to the Veneto estate, you can again take a train from Verona to the nearby town of Negrar and taxi from there if you do not hire a car. Find out more at www.tommasi.com/family/

- Masi Winery: Masi is a renowned producer of Amarone wines for you red wine lovers, comprising four estates, a cellar you can also visit, and countless Masi wine bars to their name. They offer diverse experiences to the estates or wine cellars with a tasting of several wines, including the three Masi Tupungato wines, and also a dedicated visit with wines paired with cheese - if you are a mouse in another life. For more information and bookings, contact via email on info@masitupungato.com

- Ca'del Bosco Winery: The Ca' del Bosco winery is a renowned producer of Franciacorta wines located in the town of Erbusco, about an hour's drive from Milan. Ca' del Bosco opened the doors of its wine cellars through tours designed to bring wine lovers closer to Franciacorta and impressive art and sculpture. The nearest town is Rovato, which also has a small train station to get there by train - and this is certainly worth it for art and culture fans.

While these are some of the iconic wineries in the region, I also want to share with you some off-the-beaten-track wineries and wine tour experiences in Veneto that are likely to be something a little bit different to those you find online:

*Figure 42. Veneto Regions*

- Gianni Tessari Winery - This small, family-run winery is located in the Soave region of Veneto and is known for producing exceptional Soave white wines. The winery offers guided tours of its vineyards and cellars, as well as tastings of its wines paired with local cheeses and other snacks. Gianni Tessari is at Via Prandi 10, Roncà (VR) 37030 and phone +39 045 7460070 or email office@giannitessari.wine

- Ca' Lustra Winery - Ca' Lustra is a boutique winery located in the Colli Euganei region of Veneto and is known for producing high-quality red and white wines. The winery offers guided tours of its vineyards and cellars, as well as tastings of its wines paired with local delicacies.

- Villa Spinosa Winery - Villa Spinosa is a historic winery located in the Valpolicella region of Veneto, and is known for producing exceptional signature Amarone and Valpolicella wines. The winery offers guided tours of either the vineyards or the cellars, as well as tastings included in both. Tours for individuals and for groups are available by appointment and conducted in Italian, English as well as German. The wine shop is open to all for tastings and purchases without reservation every day, too - hoorah. Call for more information at either +39 045 7500093 or +39 340 3060480

- Fattoria La Maliosa - This small, organic winery in the Lessinia region of Veneto is known for producing unique wines made using ancient grape varieties. Fattoria La Maliosa offers a huge range of experiences and is forward-thinking in its approach, as it can be booked with vouchers available online and customised entirely via the e-shop. The tours can include picnics on either the Skydeck, a large 'table d'orientation' with a panoramic view of the Tuscan Maremma hills or a lunch-style picnic among the vineyards and olive groves. Children even have a mini-picnic basket specifically made for them, and most wineries, I wouldn't say, normally win any awards for being 'child-friendly', so this is a nice touch here. Reservations are required for all tours and picnics and can be made online at www.fattorialamaliosa.it/en/

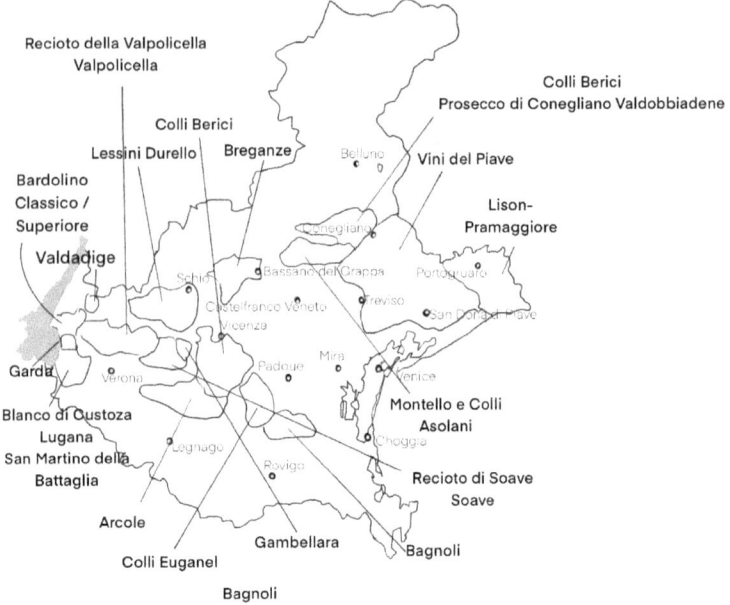

*Figure. 43 Veneto Wine Regions*

Perhaps Veneto's most glorious wine experience is the Prosecco Road - if only all roads led here, right? The Prosecco Road is a wine experience that takes visitors through the picturesque hills of the Prosecco region of Veneto.

Remember in Lombardy, we covered the difference between the sparkling wines of Northern Italy? Well, here we are, where Prosecco is produced in these regions of Veneto, whereas Franciacorta is only produced in Lombardy *(Lake Como for you, 2022)*

On this divine drive, there are more than 30 vineyards of Prosecco through and through - most of them small and family-run, and it's the area that produces the best in Italy. As well as all those bubbles, in this area, you'll find the unusual and delicious Prosecco 'Liscio' – a still version of the wine. *(Rosemary and Pork Belly, 2022)*

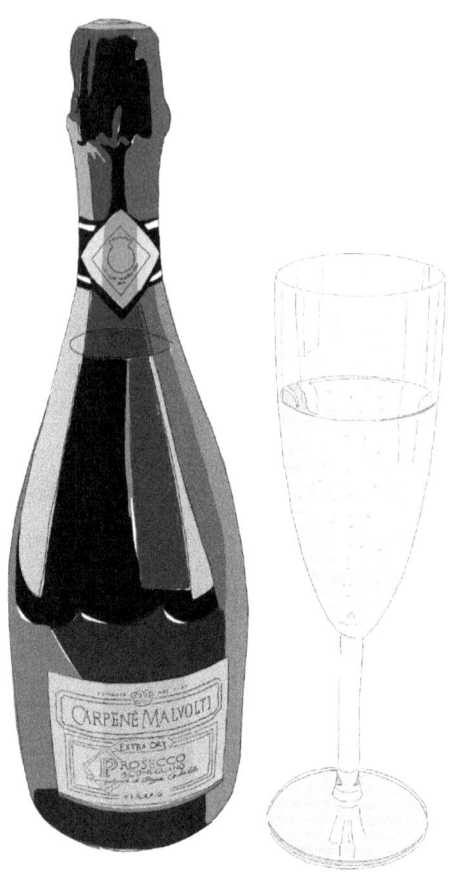

*Figure 44. Prosecco*

You will find it on local menus in this area, and it is rare even across Italy, let alone anywhere else in the world. Once you've toasted this rare delight, you can stop at as many wineries as you like, indulge in tastings of classic bubbly Prosecco wines, and have the chance to learn about the history and culture of the region. Begin or end at the small town of Valdobbiadene and end at Conegliano, or the other way around, and don't worry too much about the route in between as there are several branches of vineyards and much discussion on what the 'official' Prosecco Road is - if you can still see, smell and taste the bubbles, then you're on the right track in my eyes.

Depending on whether you start or end there, Valdobbiadene, at one end of the trail, is known as the capital of Prosecco and offers a variety of unique wine experiences beyond the well-known wineries and even the expected wine experiences elsewhere in Italy. It is here I want you to save some of your energy and, let's face it, €, for some of the most outstanding, lesser-known wine experiences to try in and around this quaint little town:

- Osteria Senz'oste: This is a truly unique wine bar in the heart of Valdobbiadene, which you must photograph and see to believe. The bar translates as 'inn without a host' *(Rosemary and Pork Belly, 2022)* and in essence, you can buy chilled Prosecco from a vending machine which operates on an honesty system - customers help themselves to a glass of Prosecco from the wine dispenser and pay on their way out. *Would this be successful everywhere?* I hear you ask... No, probably not. But Valdobbiadene isn't everywhere, and somehow, the people and the Prosecco are all just better here.

- The Prosecco Cycle Route: Imagine the Prosecco Road, but the mad version for people in lycra. Jokes aside, be careful of the cycling and prosecco combo, but apart from that, it is simply glorious and a cycling trail that takes visitors through the vineyards and hills of this breathtaking region. The trail starts and ends in Valdobbiadene, much like the road driven by the far lazier drivers, and offers stunning views of the landscape and opportunities to stop at local wineries along the way with the gift of two wheels rather than four with the wind blowing in your hair.

- Agriturismo La Vigna: This is a charming agriturismo area of winemaking located just outside of the town of Valdobbiadene, which offers a variety of activities, including vineyard tours, wine tastings and cooking classes featuring local ingredients. We don't have an equivalent to it in England or the US, and you find certain areas of outstanding natural beauty in Italy.

- La Cima del Colle: This is a winery located in the hills of Valdobbiadene, and offers a unique wine-tasting experience in a 16th-century watchtower. If you don't like heights, then just... well, don't. Otherwise, this is a unique chance to taste a variety of Prosecco wines from the top of your watchtower while enjoying panoramic views of the surrounding landscape and trying not to drop your phone.

- Villa Sandi - This historic villa is located just outside of Valdobbiadene, and is known for its outstanding Prosecco wines. The villa offers guided tours of its vineyards and cellars, as well as tastings of its wines paired with local cheeses and snacks.

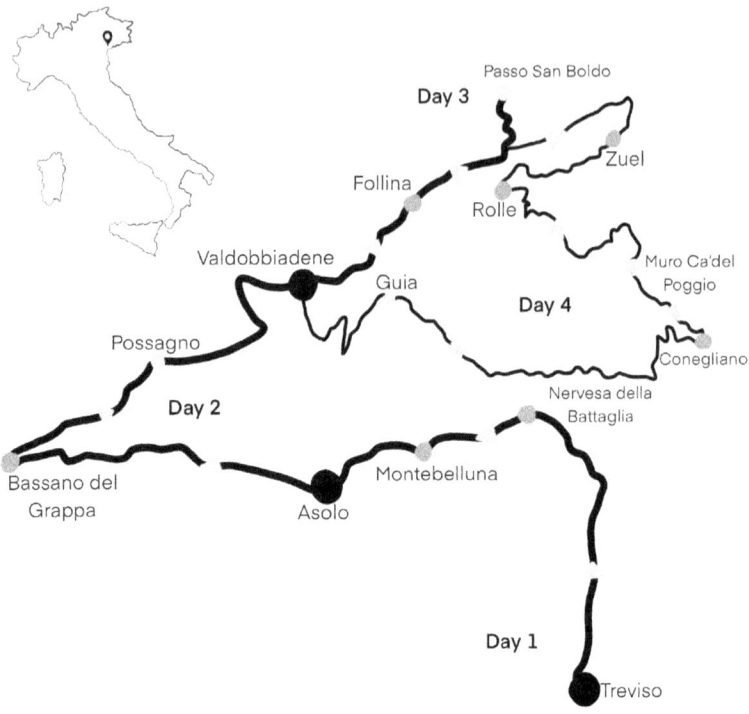

*Figure 45. Prosecco Cycle Route*

Overall, the charm in the Veneto region for me is the chance to get off the beaten track and explore the lesser-known corners of this beautiful, otherwise well-known region. If you have time, then tick off a big winery or two and then get yourself to the charm of Valdobbiadene and the Prosecco Road for less tourists, more local wines, and a unique glimpse into the wine culture of the Prosecco region.

## Summary of Chapter 4

I hope this chapter has given you a good idea of what you can see and do in these Northern Italian wine regions and the main types of wines to try. We first dived into the Piemonte region, known for its prestigious wines, including Barolo and Barbaresco - from the Nebbiolo grape. Visit the Langhe hills, where the region's wine production is concentrated and where the microclimates and altitudes make it perfect for grapevines and your rustic wine experiences. The nearby Roero area is another to explore picturesque vineyards, taste these bold red wines, and indulge in the region's renowned culinary delights.

Moving down to Lombardy, we learned the region is home to the Franciacorta area, famous for its sparkling wines made using the traditional method and what that means you can expect to see.

Explore the vineyards, visit renowned wineries, taste the bubbles, and enjoy tasting all the Franciacorta wines you can. Additionally, in the Valtellina region, try the other Nebbiolo-based red wines known as Chiavennasca.

In the Veneto region and the cultural offerings, we explored how the area offers a variety of uniquely Italian wine experiences. It is here you must ride the wonderfully-named Prosecco Road, and I hope I provided some of the best stop-offs in the surrounding charming areas near Valdobbiadene and the unusual wine experiences to make a beeline for, as well as the bigger, well-known wineries of an iconic Northern wine region like Veneto.

This isn't to say there isn't far more to explore in the Northern Italian wine regions - other regions well worth visiting and with exceptional wines include Friuli-Venezia Giulia, in particular Collio and Colli Orientali del Friuli areas for white wine tours, as well as excellent reds from grapes like Merlot, Cabernet Franc and Refosco. The Trentino-Alto Adige region is also known for its alpine landscapes and cool-climate wines. Here, visit the iconic vineyards along the Wine Road and taste the region's renowned whites, including Pinot Grigio and Sauvignon Blanc.

Hopefully, the regions we cover in detail in this chapter have given you a good understanding of not just the wines and tours on offer but also the beautiful landscapes, lesser-known wine experiences and historical or culinary delights to capture along the way. Whether you're exploring wineries on a formal tour of the North, slightly tipsy cycling through vineyards, or just enjoying wine with local Italian cuisine, the wine regions of northern Italy provide a really enriching experience for wine lovers and travellers alike - and Salute to the best bits of the North before we travel further down the country together.

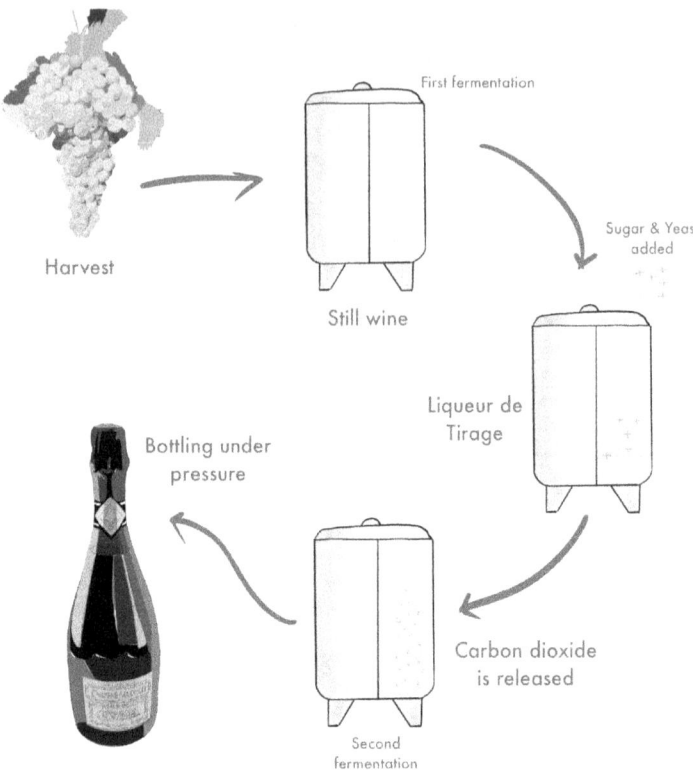

*Figure 46. Marinotti Method for Making Prosecco*

# PLEASE REVIEW THIS BOOK!

If you enjoy this book, we would be so grateful to hear your thoughts! Your reviews are not only a source of motivation for us as authors but also invaluable for other readers looking for their next great read. Sharing your feedback can help us reach more book lovers like you. Please take a moment to leave a short review and share your experience with us, it makes such a huge difference! Thank you for being a part of our wine journey!

CHAPTER 5

# TOUR OF CENTRAL ITALY'S WINE REGIONS

Moving downwards in the country, for our friends and readers looking to explore the middle regions, the definition of 'Central Italy' most certainly exists. Despite this, there is a tendency to split the country merely between Northern and Southern Italy and can still be confusing when planning a trip there. Therefore, let's be clear from the outset that the area of Central Italy, for this purpose, can be defined as the six regions of Tuscany, Lazio, Marche, Abruzzo, Umbria and Molise - in no particular order. The diagram below will help to refresh your memory of where these regions sit in relation to each other and the wider country borders.

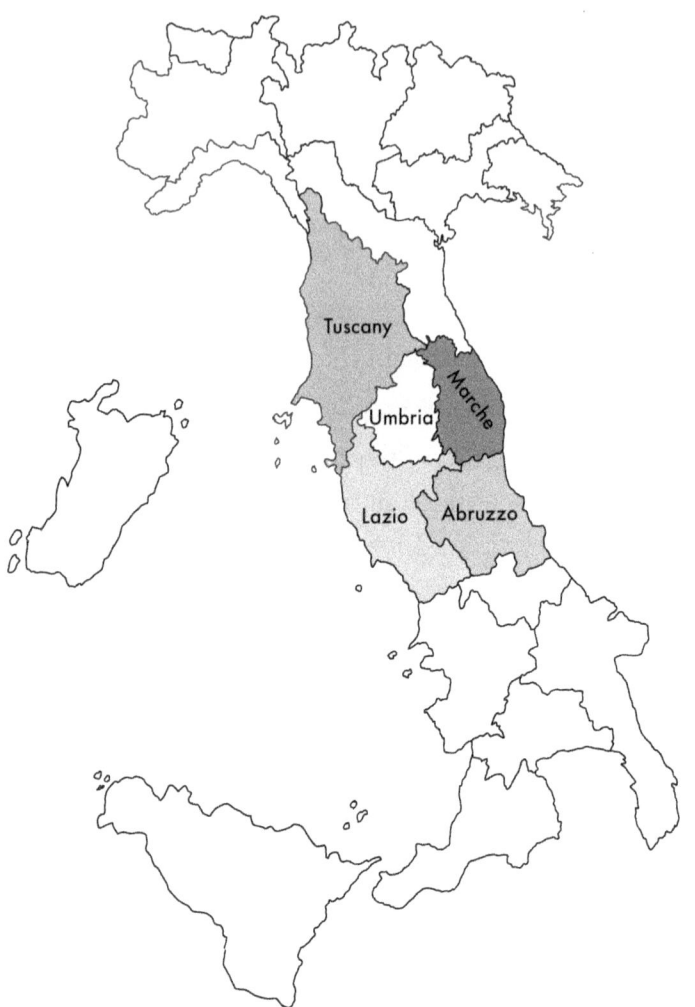

*Figure 47. Central Italy*

The area outlined above as Central Italy, encompasses a range of landscapes - from the rolling hills of Tuscany to the Apennine Mountains and the coastal areas of Le Marche. This diversity creates a wide array of microclimates and soil types and it provides varying conditions for growing different grape varieties and a huge variety of wine styles.

Central Italy also has a rich historical and cultural heritage that has had a great influence on its wine scene. The region is home to iconic cities such as Florence, which played a pivotal role in the Renaissance; Rome, need I say more, and; Assisi, associated with St. Francis.

This historical legacy contributes to the wine culture and traditions of the region we see so clearly in the wines produced and how they are enjoyed. Its wine scene can be characterised by its diversity as well as its historical significance and a strong sense of authenticity. These distinctions make it the perfect destination for wine lovers seeking exceptional wines and the truly, shamelessly Italian, rich cultural experience.

Of the six central regions, Tuscany covers the largest geographical region with approximately 22,985 km² *(Italy Review, 2022)*, and thanks to the capital city of Rome, with its six million inhabitants sitting with the region of Lazio instead, it is there that has the largest population. *(Italy Review, 2022)*

Since Rome itself is an entire other book's worth of incredible recommendations for its wine scene and bars - and if you're very lucky I am sure we will have released a Rome Travel Journal and Colouring Book for this very reason - I have decided not to cover Lazio in its own right to avoid the risk of not doing it justice in a sweeping regional tour.

There are plenty of amazing books and sources to use for Rome alone and its gastronomical delights, and you will find plenty online for a city break. Looking at the wider region briefly, it is an exciting time for Lazio in that the region has been seeing some incredible, innovative wine projects popping up, including a promotion of Latina wines via the Strada del Vino project, and the innovative wineries in this space such as Cincinnato. *(La Vita Roma, 2020)* We will also be sure to support all the projects we can of this kind, on social media.

For the above reason, we will go forth with exploring in greater depth the famed heart of central Italy's wine country, Tuscany, instead - as well as the regions of Le Marche; which lies to the east of Tuscany and faces out onto the Adriatic Coast, and Umbria; which is the smallest regions of central Italy and only one of the six to be completely landlocked.

The Central Italy cluster of six regions, as you can see above, also comprises Abruzzo, which is fairly rugged as a region and is characterised by its undulating vineyard landscapes and hinterland *(Italy Review, 2022)* and Molise, which was once part of a larger region called The Abruzzi along with the modern-day Abruzzo (now separated).

Molise has a small stretch of coastline on the Adriatic Coast and a varied hinterland of forest and plains. Before skipping past these regions, if this is where you have your heart set, then pack your walking boots and get a hiking guide in addition to some wine knowledge!

But if I can give a shout-out to some great spots here before hop-skipping off, then Emidio Pepe is a family-owned winery in Abruzzo, famous for its traditional and age-worthy Montepulciano d'Abruzzo wines and this is a must-try label from the whole region. And Molise, which has a growing wine scene focusing on indigenous grape varieties, has a great winery called Di Majo Norante, which produces a wide range of wines, but notably, the native red grape Tintilia, which you are unlikely to find in many other spots.

Now, back on track to the regions we will cover…the below examples of the Central Italian wineries are deeply rooted in local traditions and a strong connection to the ancient land. Many wineries are still family-owned and produce wines using traditional methods passed down through generations. It is this charm and aged traditions that make even the most commercial areas of the central wine country still authentic.

The centre of Italy has remained post-card beautiful, and the emphasis on authenticity contributes to the experiences you will have there and the wine you enjoy from the land.

## Tuscany

It is hard to even know where to start with Tuscany; the breath of this region is too vast and there will always be more to see and more wines to try! A Tuscan wine tour won't be an impulse stop at a few roadside wine bars - it's a truly immersive experience of one of the most famous wine regions in the world, from its undulating hills to the ruins of mediaeval churches and the landscapes that inspired Leonardo da Vinci. *(Decanter, 2021)*

Before we even get to the wines, Tuscany offers incredible landscapes and charming towns by the dozen at every turn. Just an afternoon's drive around the rolling Tuscan hills is practically therapy.

The hills of Chianti and the coastal area of Bolgheri all sit within this Italian gem of a region, and the rugged landscapes of Montalcino are the greatest appeal that keeps me coming back again and again to Tuscany.

Food, naturally, is a big part of the wine-tasting culture here, so expect to do some first-hand 'research' on Tuscan wine and food pairings wherever you visit.

Much like its European counterparts, this flagship wine region of Italy is internationally renowned for the most exceptional wines, particularly the famous red wines we know and love across the world, such as Chianti, Brunello di Montalcino and Vino Nobile di Montepulciano, to name just a few.

These wines are made from indigenous grape varieties like Sangiovese and have gained global recognition for their quality and ageing potential in perfect conditions. Sangiovese is the backbone of Tuscan winemaking and is responsible for producing wines with a distinct combination of elegance and acidity.

The region's winemaking tradition dates back to ancient times, with evidence of grape cultivation and wine production as early as the Etruscan era, covered like a mini history lesson in my previous book, The Italian Wine Connoisseur. "When the Greeks first arrived in their boot-shaped heaven in the 8th century BC, they brought with them, I assume in addition to a pretty feral boat, the true art of winemaking as we know it today. In fact, the Mycenaean Greeks have been attributed to this technique in all its glory, introducing viticulture first to Sicily and then to Southern Italy. They honed their winemaking prowess as a matter of urgency and nicknamed the land that had so impressed them, "Oenotria," or 'the land of trained vines' in English" *(The Italian Wine Connoisseur, 2022)*

Tuscany's winemaking prowess was then further enhanced during the Middle Ages, when noble families and monasteries invested in vineyards and refined the winemaking techniques.

The most famous Tuscan wine varietals of note today, and to certainly look for during a wine tour, include:

- Chianti: Chianti is perhaps the most iconic Tuscan wine, produced primarily from Sangiovese grapes. It is known for its cherry flavours, balanced acidity and medium body.

Chianti comes in various styles, including the traditional Chianti Classico. You can stay in the charming city of Florence, just a short drive from Chianti country, where you will find wineries with Michelin-starred restaurants, or relax within luxurious resorts nearby.

*Figure 48. Chianti Wine*

- Brunello di Montalcino: Produced in the town of Montalcino, it is made exclusively from Sangiovese Grosso grapes. These wines are characterised by a rich, full-bodied nature and intense flavours of dark fruits. They are renowned for their ageing potential and also famous the world over.

- Vino Nobile di Montepulciano: Produced in the town of Montepulciano, this is another wine made primarily from Sangiovese grapes, locally known as Prugnolo Gentile. Vino Nobile di Montepulciano wines are known for their complexity, structure, and ageing potential.

- Super Tuscans: In the late 20th century, Tuscany gained further recognition with the emergence of Super Tuscans. These challenged traditional winemaking regulations by blending Sangiovese with international grape varieties - such as Cabernet Sauvignon and Merlot. Super Tuscans are known for their exceptional quality, richness and complexity.

Winery tours or even entire Tuscany holidays can take on the holiday of a lifetime experience. In wineries like Antinori (travelling from Florence), Frescobaldi and Castello Banfi wineries are all truly exceptional, world-renowned experiences of wine estates.

If you choose a globally recognised winery of this kind, you will find many options online for booking. An option is to be picked up from Florence to Antinori winery, for example, and tour companies like Viator offer a private car from a city office, where you meet your driver, a local guide and your wine expert, who stays with you for the duration of the tour.

Heading firstly to Cantina Antinori, the Antinori family has been in the wine business since 1385 and at their new headquarters, you will find a historic and prolific wine empire that boasts two of Italy's top wines: Tignanello and Solaia, produced on the iconic Antinori estate. *(Decanter, 2021)* First opened in August 2013, the winery building was designed by leading Italian architect Marco Casamonti and has more than 600 years of winemaking on display within its wine museum. *(Decanter, 2021)*

Getting there will take you to the village of Bargino in the Chianti hills, and you certainly can't miss the building that the architect designed for this prestigious winemaker. *(New York Times, 2013)* The unique and impressive building has cushions on a hill, and once inside, you are warmly welcomed to try all the different types of wine and listen to stories and anecdotes about the Antinori family and a legacy spanning centuries.

An experience like this feels truly genuine even on a large scale- it's one of the wineries where you are invited to walk through the vineyards, visit the cellars, and are guided throughout. Knowledgeable guides and family members take turns sharing the winery's history, winemaking techniques, and the unique characteristics of their wines. *(Viator, 2023)* Wine tastings include iconic wines like Tignanello, Solaia their famous Chianti Classico, and other Tuscan varietals.

On-site Lunch is a delight on the top floor in the restaurant 'Rinuccio 1180,' where chef Matteo Cambi cooks a perfect 'Chianti burger.' *(Decanter, 2021)* Other Tuscan dishes are prepared with locally sourced ingredients here, and the food is chosen perfectly with the accompanying wines, as you'd expect. If using a travel agent specialising in the best of the area, you might have lunch off-site and try "La Cantinetta di Rignana" restaurant instead - this is a restaurant for people in the know on the wine scene here and is halfway between the Antinori vineyard and the Brolio Castle. Here is a heavenly selection of local salamis, cheeses, Tuscan crostini, extra-virgin olive oil, pasta and meat dishes, accompanied by wines and local products - you are quite literally living the Italian dream in every mouthful.

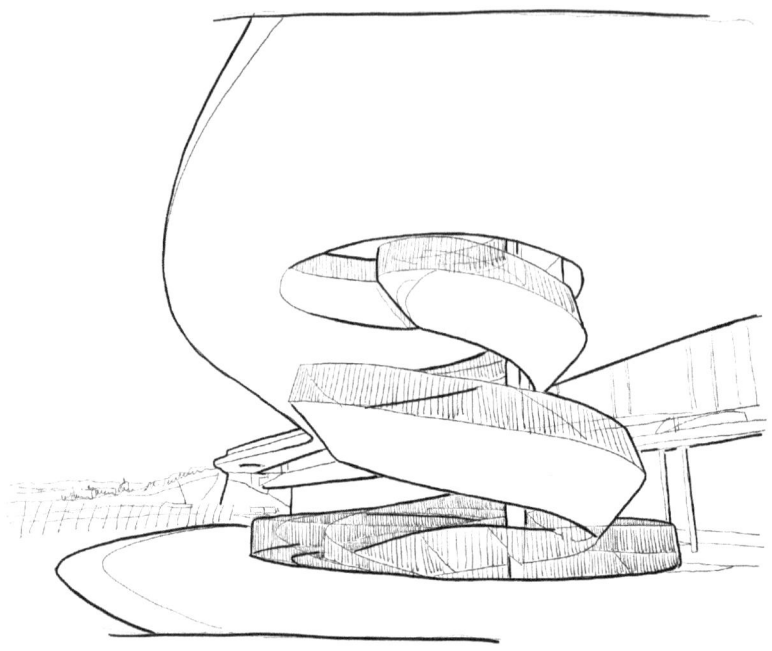

*Figure 49. Cantina Antinori*

The image above shows the impressive architecture of the estate. Outside, the panoramic terrace is shaded by a gorgeous canopy under rows of vines. Now, I won't dwell on the delight of Antinori for too much longer, I promise, but as one of my favourite wineries in Italy, its aura can't be understated.

The fact that it is owned by such a noble family with winemaking roots dating back 26+ generations *(New York Times 2013)* is what makes it feel truly historical. The Antinoris have occupied one of the great palaces in Florence since 1506 *(New York Times 2013)*, so if you come here from the big smoke of Florence, you also make an immediate link between the ostentatious palace and the stunning company headquarters.

It is a place that truly has an impact, and yes, it is now a huge exporter of wines, but it has remained true to its history and family heritage, and a day spent here is more of a cultural immersion than just a few glasses of wonderful wine. Read more about Antinori Winery & Brolio Castle private tour on websites like  or see more below for general information:

Hours and visits: Open every day from 9.30 am to 6 pm. Guided tours run every hour (10 am–4 pm) for €35 per person. Booking is essential if you would like the tour in English, and custom tour options are also available. There are several casual tasting options for those visiting without reservations. The top tour, Bottaia Cru, takes two-and-a-half hours and includes lunch at the Rinuccio 1180 restaurant with wine matching. Address and Contact: Via Cassia per Siena 133, 50026 Bargino, San Casciano in Val di Pesa. +39 055 2359700;

Frescobaldi is the next esteemed Tuscan winery with a long and famed winemaking heritage. Frescobaldi embodies the essence of Tuscany, its viticulture and the diversity of its territories. *(, 2023)* Frescobaldi's empire spans nine properties across Tuscany, including The Castello Nipozzano, a castle territory dating back to 1000 close to the Tuscan Apennines, and set in the prestigious Chianti Rufina area. It was an ancient defensive stronghold of Florence and the most celebrated and historic property of the Frescobaldi family and their wine empire.

It is said that the foresight of an ancestor of the Frescobaldi family led to an 1855 investment of 1,000 florins to begin the cultivation of grape varieties previously unknown in Tuscany, such as Cabernet Sauvignon, Merlot, Cabernet Franc and Petit Verdot. *(, 2023)* After over a century of care and cultivation, these vines produce the great wine of its famous wine estate, Mormoreto.

You can schedule a wine-tasting visit directly here and enjoy a tour of the castle and the cellars, take a walk among hundreds of acres of vines facing the Arno River valley, and enjoy sampling wines such as Sangiovese and Toscano IGT right up to the Chianti Rufina Riserva DOCG. *(Summer in Italy, 2022)*

You can also reserve a lunch expertly prepared to pair with the wine tasting. It is best to reserve it all online at the Castello Nipozzano website or see if tour guides offer the package for a similar price and include other local wine destinations you may like to see.

*Figure 50. Castello Nipozzano*

Another of the Frescobaldi's amazing properties is the Tenuta Castiglioni, which has been in the family since the 11th century. The estate extends along the ancient Via di Castiglioni, built by the Romans to unify northern Tuscany and Rome. This area just outside of Florence has been famous for the quality of its agricultural harvests for centuries, and the 700 years of wine-making history began at this very estate. Here, you can try their famous red wines, including Giramonte and Castiglioni - each estate sharing the bottlings from their own vines.

Across all of its properties, Frescobaldi prides itself on the passion of its agronomists and oenologists, who, thanks to the history and family heritage, are dedicated and qualified experts in the vineyards and terroirs of the many sprawling estates. The family and winemakers live by the respect for traditions, for Tuscany, for its land and work hard with a unique combination of soil, altitude and microclimates to deliver their famous varietals.

The other charm of the Frescobaldi properties is the combination of art and wine. You may have the opportunity to appreciate specialised art collections, exhibitions, and certainly historic architecture as part of your visit to some of these estates, and read carefully about where to see before booking your visit if you intend to take in the impressive collections. More information on all of the estates at

While in Northern Tuscany, another winery that is truly historic and a must-do while in the region, is Capezzana, at which a winery visit includes the most iconic cellar tour with the traditional wines on show from the Carmignano DOCG. *(Decanter, 2021)*

Just a few miles from Florence, in the direction of Prato, the incredible Capezzena estate has been producing wine and extra-virgin olive oil since 1804. More recently, the Contini Bonaccossi family has been running the estate since the 1920s, and currently, a young generation of the family has expertly taken the helm and created the newest aspect of the winery: a wine bar called La Vinsantaia (open from April–October each year) where guests enjoy informal wine tastings and food. *(Decanter, 2021)*

This really changes the scope of a wine tasting here and makes a friendly version of a tasting experience that would otherwise be lost in the sweeping estate, with 650 hectares of forest, organic vineyards and olive groves, and a renowned cookery school. *(Decanter, 2021)*

In the summer months, sat here, you can enjoy the terrace with more than just a decent skyline - you are looking straight at the view of Florence's Duomo in the distance and can be sipping on one of Tuscany's greatest wines – the Vin Santo, a dessert wine made from grapes left to turn to raisins on drying racks and sweet enough to rival even the finest decadent dessert.

*Figure 51. Il Duomo in Florence*

Capezzana is open from Monday to Saturday throughout the year. Tours start from €20 per person for a tour and wine tasting with three wines to try. Booking in advance is recommended, and the contact details to arrange directly with the winery are address: Via Capezzana 100, 59015 Carmignano; phone +39 055 8706005 and online at

Moving to Brunello di Montalcino wines of the Montalcino area of Tuscany, these are highly regarded for their quality, elegance and ability to express the area's terroir. Brunello di Montalcino is considered one of Italy's most prestigious and long-standing red wines, made exclusively from Sangiovese grapes mentioned above, locally known as 'Sangiovese Grosso.' Brunello wines are required by law to be aged for a minimum of 5 years, with at least 2 years in oak barrels, resulting in intense flavours of red and dark fruits, such as cherry, plum and blackberry. Tasting these wines on-site at wineries across Montalcino allows for the sweetest of appreciation if this is one of your faves.

A winery that stands out for this is the last of our three 'super-recommendations' in Tuscany - Castello Banfi, set in the Montalcino area and also known for its prestigious Brunello di Montalcino wines. A visit to Castello Banfi il Borgo includes a site with a hotel, two restaurants, the Enoteca, the Balsameria and the Glass Museum, heaven for wine lovers!

It is a multi-experience day, where you could stay from dusk until dawn in a unique site immersed in one of the most beautiful places in the world. You can explore the vineyards and cellars, learn about sustainable winemaking practices and traditional techniques, and then enjoy everything the site offers.

Sustainability efforts are really something to shout about here -and for those of you interested in our changing world and how to support those making efforts in transformation, Banfi firmly believes in sustainability as a comprehensive concept across their supply chain, adopting a dedicated strategy and production plans. *(2023)*

As a brand, Banfi has always cared about the environment and consumer wellness from its origins. By releasing a transparent sustainability report each year and through a rationalised use of natural resources and a love for the environment, the winery is evidence of care and dedication from the vineyards to the final bottle of wine produced. *(2023)* Over the last couple of decades, Banfi has participated in low-input cultivation by carefully monitoring fertilisation and focusing on low-persistence ingredients that are gentle to the environment. They make other efforts you can see on site, like ratios of forest to cultivated land, planting local species of trees, and providing drinking water for wildlife. The feel-good factor is incredible... as is the wine!

Tastings here and the best experience of the wines and gastronomy for me have to be in the Enecote (or wine bar to you and i) - this is the more casual of the settings here, where the atmosphere of a true Tuscan wine shop has been replicated and where, alongside the estate's best still and sparkling wines, you can try grappa, extra virgin olive oil and Condimento Balsamico Etrusco, as well as buy numerous local artisan food and crafts.

Their finest wine varieties to try and then take home from the shop include Brunello di Montalcino and Rosso di Montalcino. Expert sommeliers here know their stuff, sharing insights into the characteristics and nuances of each wine and talking with precision and interest about their fine bottlings and care for the environment.

*Figure 52. Banfi Il Borgo*

If you leave Banfi needing more, there are, and will always be, several more outstanding wineries nearby that are top-quality and well-worth visiting, even if slightly lower-key and smaller in size.

To experience the renowned Brunello di Montalcino wines, some of the other best wineries to see in the Montalcino area of Tuscany include the following:

- Biondi-Santi: Biondi-Santi is an iconic winery credited with creating Brunello di Montalcino. They have a long-standing winemaking tradition and produce age-worthy wines. The winery offers guided tours and tastings, providing insights into their winemaking methods and the history of Brunello. You can find out more here: www.biondisanti.it

- Il Poggione: Il Poggione is a family-owned winery with a rich history dating back to the late 19th century. They are highly regarded for their traditional winemaking approach and produce exemplary Brunello di Montalcino wine.

The winery selects the best French oak to be used for its ageing process and since it is completely underground, the cellar's temperature and humidity are naturally ideal, providing perfect storage for the wine. You can reach Tenuta Il Poggione by email at info@ilpoggione.it or by phone on +39 0577 844 029 at 53024 Montalcino, Siena.

- Col d'Orcia is one of the largest wineries in the famed Montalcino area and is owned by the Cinzano family of the famous Vermouth name. It is an old-fashioned, organic farm with a tasting room, a dining room table, and family paintings on the wall - a world away from some of the large commercial wineries we have covered so far in Tuscany if this is more your vibe.

Col d'Orcia is located down the Montalcino hill, opposite the impressive Banfi mentioned above. It also has a lovely visitor offering, including luxury accommodation in the adjacent castle complex. *(Decanter, 2021)*

A tour here takes you around the organic wine-producing farm, followed by a tasting in a space that feels like the Cinzano family dining room. Wines you will get to try include a Tuscan Pinot Grigio, Sant'Antimo and Brunello - including an array of back-vintages the family will get out for the occasion.

Hours and visits: Various types of visits can be arranged starting from €15 per person. Booking beforehand is recommended, especially for food options, as it does not have a restaurant, but they are happy to cook for parties who would like lunch or dinner. Address and Contact: Località Via Giuncheti, 53024 Montalcino SI, Italy. +39 0577 80891;

These wineries all provide immersive wine experiences and outstanding varietals that showcase their rich history, winemaking expertise, and the unique terroir of Montalcino. The specific offerings may vary at each one, and it can depend on the season and the droves of tourist numbers at certain times of the year, so it's recommended to check websites directly or contact the wineries via email or phone to inquire about the tour availability, tasting options and any special experiences you want to try.

Moving to a few other wineries in different areas of Tuscany, Monteverro is a fairly new project that we have read a lot about but not yet visited (as of the summer of 2023 - give us time!) It has been built around the owner's original love of Bordeaux varietals – don't tell a motivated wine producer they can't recreate what has been done brilliantly in France!

In the Southern tip of Tuscany, an hour south of Grosseto near Monte Argentario and Tuscany's best beaches, you find Capalbio, which is home to the wine project started in 2003 by Julia and Georg Weber. *(Decanter, 2021)*

Here, you are welcomed through cast iron gates into a series of very Tuscan buildings paying homage to the local wild boar, lending its name to the property. Seriously more refined than any further boar references, once inside the wine-making facilities and barrel rooms, they are pristine and evoke a far older and well-established wine operation.

A Monteverro wine tour can be arranged by contacting them in advance and it costs €65 to try 6 wines. *(Decanter, 2021)* It starts with a tour of the bug hotel, a structure designed to help bring insects to the vineyards and create a novelty nature experience that we are all likely to appreciate, followed by a walk around the vines on the rolling Tuscan hills. You will then be guided through the wine-making facilities and onto the barrel and tasting rooms. *(Decanter, 2021)*

This site will hugely appeal to those who have been to Bolgheri and seek the vibe of a modern vision for the wine scene. It is also a great choice for those wanting to witness a family's ambition to create world-class wine and who want to hear the stories and vision behind how they achieved it.

Hours and visits: Booking beforehand is required. For an additional €15 on the €65, you can add a plate of local cheese, ham and other Tuscan fare to your tasting, a great way to tick off lunch as well. Address and Contact: Monteverro Srl Società Agricola Strada Aurelia Capalbio 11 I-58011 Capalbio (GR) Phone +39 564 890721 and email info@monteverro.com

*Figure 53. Monteverro Wild Boar*

For those who think they might like a taste of all the above and more, then I suggest a longer, dedicated, elaborate regional tour of a few days around Tuscany might be the answer. I am not sure that has ever not appealed to anyone...

If you have the time and the budget, then companies like *Meet Piemonte Tours*, which we looked at in Northern Italy, also offer a wide range of tour options in the Central Tuscany region. The most delicious of which is the longest, 9-day small group grand tour, which we highly recommend for those with more days to spare (lucky things) and who want to discover all the must-sees and highlights of Italy's most popular wine region in one easy-to-plan holiday. It allows you to travel with a small group, always limited to 12 guests, for an intimate and well-planned journey travelling in style across Tuscany from the wine region of Val D'Orcia to the beaches of Viareggio, then from Carrara's marble quarries to the buzz of the Mediterranean coastline. *(Meet Piemonte Tours, 2022)*

This tour will set you back a few thousand €, sure, but if you're looking to have everything planned for you and to sweep from Pienza, Montalcino, San Gimignano, and Pisa over to the abbey of St. Antimo, and all the time skipping the queues for the landmarks included in the tour, then this is for you!

You only have to get to the Accademia Museum in Florence to try and see the original David by Michelangelo to know you would do anything for the queue jump alone!

The tour also includes culinary delights and is all set in a Tuscan countryside luxury villa surrounded by olive trees and vineyards.

See more on their website for details and the general map route below:

# THE ITALIAN WINE TOUR POCKET GUIDE

*Figure 54. Montecuco Wine Trail*

Many other wine tour companies will offer similar planned tours in Tuscany for a week plus. Alternatively, if you want to escape the tourists in Tuscany rather than join them, you could try the Montecucco wine trail - one of the most serene experiences for wine enthusiasts and travellers seeking wineries and guided tours on a more peaceful trail where you'll learn about the winemaking process, vineyard management practices, and the unique characteristics of Montecucco wines but without the crowds. Set in the Southern corner of Tuscany, the trail spreads between Morellino di Scansano to the South and Brunello di Montalcino to the North-East. Cinigiano, Civitella Paganico, Campagnatico, Castel del Piano, Roccalbenga and Arcidosso are among the communities in the Grosseto province that make up the Montecucco wine region *(Wine Tourism, 2023)* and are your stop-offs for delicious local everyday wines and delicacies on route as well as the larger wineries.

The area is known worldwide for its Sangiovese-based red wines and is regarded as a hidden treasure in the world of wine for those in the know. It is one of Italy's newest districts on the wine map, established in 1998 and an area where the new-world organic vine cultivation accounts for two-thirds of total vineyards. *(Wine Tourism, 2023)*

Some wineries offer food and wine pairing 'premier tasting' experiences, where you can enjoy traditional dishes prepared using locally sourced ingredients, perfectly paired with the region's wines. There are also often wine festivals and events taking place along the trail - so check the calendars and tie it in if you want to experience a truly authentic Italian *festa*!

These events provide opportunities to taste a wide range of wines, participate in workshops or masterclasses and immerse yourself in the vibrant wine culture. If you are looking for a specific stop-off at a winery, the below are my favourites from my research and experience - all costing between €15 - €25 (as of 2023) and well worth every cent:

- Tenuta Impostino winery includes a visit to a large tasting room of the winery, where the staff will offer you wines from their portfolio and pair them with lunch or dinner in the estate-owned restaurant perched on the edge of the Tuscan hills. You also see the vineyards and cellars as well as seeing and trying several of the cultivation stages. This winery's USP, which you may love or hare, is an included activity of a 4km trek along the hillside, which is free and open throughout the year - but certainly more bearable after wine tasting. For more information and bookings, https://www.torciano.com/

- Parmoleto Wine Company produces quality wines and olive oil at their farmhouse winery and estate. There are four apartments and four bedrooms to host visitors on-site - so pack your wellies and get stuck in. Or there is a swimming pool and a barbeque area for those realists among us. This is a rustic and genuine spot in Tuscany, where you enjoy a tour of the vineyards as well as seeing first-hand the farming methods and how the site runs day to day. A visit to the cellar gives a great understanding of the winemaking practises, and you top the day off with generous samples of unique, regional wines with fabulous olive oil paired with traditional Tuscan dishes and snacks. For more info and bookings, https://www.parmoleto.it/home-eng/

- Muschi Alti winery really gives you eyes on the transparent wine-making practices and tasting supply chain. The itinerary consists of a guided tour of vineyards, where guests can learn the viticulture philosophy of the Ottonelli family and a guided experience of the estate's wine production stages from fermentation through to bottling. The staff here serve you wines straight from the source, paired with local food products from the Maremma region, including delicious cold meat cuts and cheeses. For more info and bookings, https://muschialti.it/en/winery/

All of the above can be booked directly through quick booking on the website or on the wineries' individual websites.

Overall, Tuscany has a combination of world-class wines, cultural heritage, and scenic beauty that has famously and firmly established its reputation as a leading wine region. Whether exploring historic cellars, indulging in wine tastings, or soaking in the Tuscan countryside from a quieter spot like the Montecucco wine trail, a wine journey through Tuscany promises an unforgettable experience for wine enthusiasts and fans. If you can't find it here in Tuscany, you can't find it anywhere!

**Umbria**

Umbria, located in Central Italy right across the border from Tuscany, is our next spotlight Central Italy region that really offers something different - a smaller, distinct wine scene known for its elegance and character.

The region produces notable white wines such as Orvieto and Grechetto and red wines like Sagrantino di Montefalco. Umbrian wines often showcase a balance between tradition and innovation, reflecting the terroir of the area. Umbria is home to several distinct wine regions, including the Torgiano and Montefalco areas - both known for producing high-quality wines and have their own DOC (Denominazione di Origine Controllata) and DOCG (Denominazione di Origine Controllata e Garantita) appellations, which as we know means in auditing terms they are hitting the high notes.

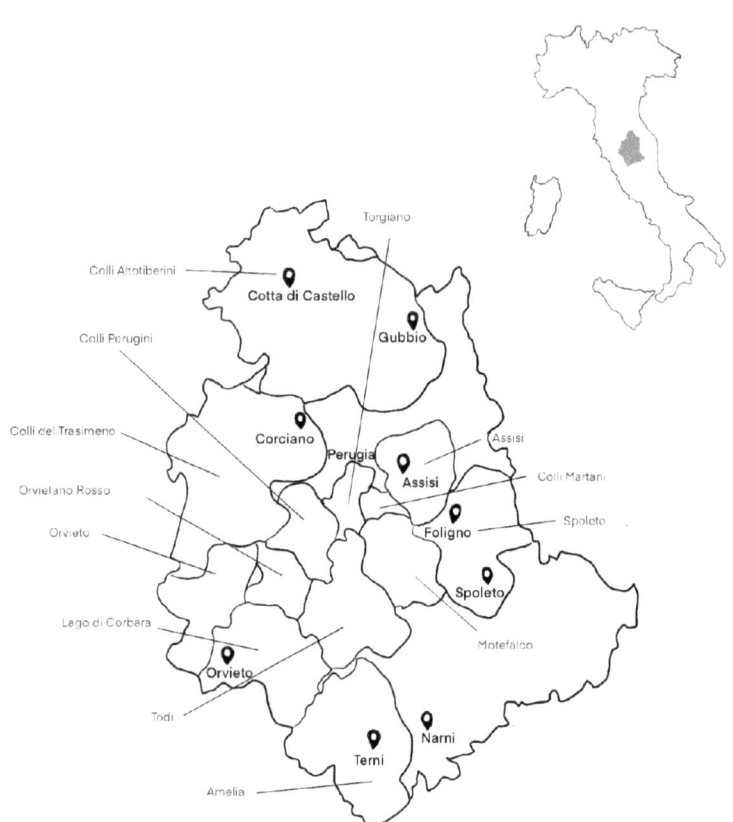

*Figure 55. Umbria Region*

The region's wine scene features a range of grape varieties, both indigenous and international. The most prominent red grape variety in Umbria is Sagrantino, which is the main grape in the prestigious above-mentioned Sagrantino di Montefalco wines that wine lovers flock to Umbria to taste.

It is one of the region's most renowned offerings and a full-bodied, age-worthy red wine with rich tannins and flavours of dark fruits and spices. Sagrantino is a bold, dry wine that is produced with the most tannic grape in Italy, the Sagrantino red grape. The wine is, therefore, no guesses here, very high in tannin and also high in acidity.

To the eye, Sagrantino is very similar to Sangiovese if this is a varietal you have loved before, but its texture is more similar to Barolo, one of our favourite 'B's' of the Italian wines covered earlier. The primary aromas in Umbria's prime red wine are those of blackberries, truffle, and earth. *(Wine Tourism, 2023)*

Other red varieties to which this also applies are Sangiovese, Merlot, and Cabernet Sauvignon. For white wines, as well as the two mentioned above, which are flagship Umbria names, the region cultivates varieties like Trebbiano and Chardonnay equally as impressively.

The best time to experience wine tastings and tours in Umbria is, like we have said before, a huge sweeping statement for anywhere in Italy, either in spring or autumn.

In Umbria's case, though, Spring is truer than anywhere else as it is when the entire region is swathed in wildflowers and sunflowers (May time), and it is like an artist's paradise or a florist's. The region is known as *'il cuore verde d'Italia'*, translated as 'the green heart of Italy,' because of its green and lavish landscapes. *(Wine Tourism, 2023)*

In the summer, temperatures rise, and the region gets crowded like elsewhere in Italy, but in Umbria, this is particularly true of the area around Assisi. This is where you will find the Cathedral of Saint Francis from Assisi, the patron saint of Italy. Tips on what to do culture-wise in the green heart of Italy, beyond exploring the wine scene, include the Orvieto Cathedral - a 13th-century Gothic and Roman cathedral; Rocca Paolina, which is a Renaissance fortress built in 1540-1543 for Pope Paul III, and; Perugia, the capital city of Umbria *(Wine Tourism, 2023)* and the Italian capital of chocolate - say no more!

Taking a moment to look at Umbrian winemakers generally, the focus is on quality production, often following traditional winemaking methods combined with modern techniques. Many wineries embrace sustainable and organic practices, respecting the environment and paving the way for the new era of wine-making and caring for the planet that has developed considerably over the last 20 years. Some of the big-name wineries include:

- Lungarotti is a renowned winery based in Turrita di Montefalco, Torgiano. It is a family-run estate that has played a significant role in promoting and elevating the wine varietals of Umbria. Lungarotti focuses on producing high-quality wines, including their iconic Torgiano Rosso Riserva and Rubesco wines, which showcase the region's indigenous grape varieties. Set in a splendid villa completely surrounded by vineyards and with unparalleled scenery, this is an incredible spot for breathtaking events, and it is the type of place that could certainly cater for a wedding or special occasion. The spacious halls, warm fireplaces and fountains make it an ideal setting for something even bigger than a wine-tasting trip - but it does that just perfectly, too!

A stop-and-sip recommendation is the Montefalco Sagrantino 2018, a heavy hitter but refined wine. This 2018 example was aged in barrels for 12 months, followed by around 20 months in the bottle. It has ripe dark fruit aromas lifted by perfumed Parma violet.

- Arnaldo Caprai is a leading winery located in Montefalco, known for its outstanding Sagrantino wines. The winery is dedicated to promoting the Sagrantino grape and its expression in both dry and sweet wines. Their Sagrantino di Montefalco DOCG wines have received critical acclaim for their complexity, structure, and ageing potential. For more info and bookings, https://www.arnaldocaprai.it/en/

Here, the winery offers four different versions of wine tours and experiences, all providing insights into their winemaking process, philosophy, and production history.

One of the experiences is the Signature Collection Experience, or the dedicated Sagrantino wine tasting, where you can sample the acclaimed Sagrantino wines. This includes a three-hour experience for a maximum of 8 people, costing € 100 per person. *(Arnoldo Caprai, 2023)*

They also offer a super cool, unusual winery experience called 'Montefalco Vibes' where you have the chance to experience the unique flavours, aromas, and structure of the Grecante, Colli Martani Grechetto DOC, Vigna Flaminia Maremmana, Montefalco Rosso DOC, and Valdimaggio, Montefalco Sagrantino DOCG wines. *(Arnoldo Caprai, 2023)*

Finally, the winery offers a classic tour and tasting experience, including tasting the above wines and five others, accompanied by a refined selection of typical local products and Umbrian gastronomy. La Terrazza Monte della Torre terrace offers unique views of Montefalco and the Sagrantino vineyards, and afterwards, you can enjoy the on-site Sagrantino Museum, showcasing the history, tradition, and cultural significance of Sagrantino. *(Arnoldo Caprai, 2023)*

Never leave a decent winery without hitting the wine shop, too! Here, you can take home some of their exceptional wines as a souvenir or enjoy once in your rainy homeland needing a pick-me-up. Arnaldo Caprai is at Località Torre, 1, 06036 Montefalco, PG,

Italy, and you can reach them by phone at +39 (0)742 378802. It is best to visit the website or contact them directly for the most up-to-date information on visiting hours, tour availability, and any specific experiences they may offer your tour group.

Next, the appellations of Torgiano Spoleto encompass the towns of Torgiano and Spoleto, both located in the heart of Umbria, which can be explored to your heart's content for those with a car and more time to play with. The area is renowned for its red wines, which we know by now, especially those made from the Sagrantino grape.

Several unique wine-tasting experiences are available throughout the region for you to discover - amazing wineries in Torgiano are open to visitors with varied, exciting booking options for tastings and tours.

You can start a tour of the entire stretch in Torgiano, 15 km from Perugia, and continue on to Bevagna, climbing up to Montefalco and finishing at Spoleto. This is an incredible route to choose if you want to cross some of the most attractive hills in Umbria and also see the main town of Perugia, where two of the Umbrian DOCG wines, the Torgiano Rosso Riserva and the Sagrantino di Montefalco, make their name. *(Somm TV, 2022)*

The winery in Piazza Onofri in Bevagna (tel. +39 0742-361926) on this route through the Umbrian heartland certainly deserves a lunch stop. It offers excellent local hosting and cuisine by the Santificetur family, who will cook up a vegetable soup, grilled beef or pork, lasagne pasta and strangozzi for you, and shower you with a wide range of wines from the region to try. *(Somm TV, 2022)*

In Foligno, the next town, we recommend the Bacco Felice (tel. +39 742-341019), which is a charming little restaurant in the historical centre destined to be a winery. If you end up needing to spend the night after a few too many local wines and organic vegetable dishes here, then Gattapone is a cute spot to lay your head, named after the architect who designed the Torri Bridge in the 1300s, and non-surprisingly whose views are admired from the rooms. *(Somm TV, 2022)*

*Figure 56. Perugia to Spoleto*

As you can see from the route map, the next logical stops would be Montefalco, within which we have visited some wineries already, and an area which claims fame for two distinctly different Umbrian red wines mentioned earlier - the Montefalco Rosso DOC, made of 70% Sangiovese and the second being the tannic, iconic Umbrian Sagrantino di Montefalco DOCG, which constitutes 100% Sagrantino. *(Somm TV, 2022)*

You can end in Spoleto, a gorgeously peaceful hill town with beautiful architecture and historical culture that remains mediaeval, with Roman ruins, including a Roman theatre and an archaeological museum worth visiting. From November to March, another town of Norcia, and Spoleto, produces famous truffles during the high season. *(Trips2Italy, 2020)* They include world-class black truffles, scorzone (available in summer), and white truffles - if you can't get the sun, at least get the best truffles, right? Along with your local glass of Orvieto white wine for a few €, you can get specialities like torta al testo (bread cooked on the marble stone in a wood-burning oven) stuffed with ham, sausage, or simply with herbs prepared fresh in olive oil. *(Trips2Italy, 2020)* Nothing like ending your mini wine tour with a full stomach and heart in the piazzo of Spoleto with your next wine adventures in mind.

Now, to look at a few more specific wineries that stand out for me in other areas of Umbria:

- Castello di Corbara is a historic winery situated near

Orvieto, close to Todi and overlooking the lake of Corbara. It is known for its commitment to sustainable agriculture, something we all love these days, and the production of quality wines. The winery produces a range of wines, including Orvieto Classico and other white blends that showcase the region's distinctive terroir, and recently, the estate has re-discovered its historical location as well as its traditions. For more info: https://castellodicorbara.it/

This estate has ancient origins and a rich and fascinating history that entices even the most uninterested of parties in anything other than wine. Since Roman times and through the Middle Ages, it was the fief of the Counts of Montemarte. *(Wine Tourism, 2023)*

Recently, the Castello di Corbara has become known for its 100 hectares of vines on over 1200 hectares of land. The vineyards were planted to take advantage of the microclimate of the individual plots of land and make the most of the wide variety of soil types in the area. The constant monitoring of the microclimate of the vineyards allows for full respect for the environment and guarantees the production of excellent wines.

The Patrizi family, with great entrepreneurial experience in wine, acquired Castello di Corbara in 1997 with the ambitious plan to relaunch the estate and its iconic wine production. *(Wine Tourism, 2023)* The wide variety of grapevines that grow here was an essential key factor for such an ambitious project to work, and the family concentrated on the many species of grapes that have been growing here for over a century, launching well-known local wines intimately linked to their terroir. Since then, the winery has been open to visitors looking to enjoy tours and tastings at their impressive site, and for as little as € 20 you can book a wine-tasting visit via Wine Tourism online or directly with the winery.

Among the reds grown here, which you get to try, Castello di Corbara promotes the production of Sangiovese and Montepulciano. A historical clone of the latter was discovered on the estate and reproduced in Spring 2003 (a very good year here!) and cleverly re-implanted in the area where the microclimate was best for the species. *(Wine Tourism, 2023)* Other reds include the Merlot, Cabernet Sauvignon and Cabernet Franc varieties, which have all given excellent results for trying here, as they have been grown on the estate lands for years and grapes are perfectly accustomed to the soils.

As for the whites, the winery proudly produces and labels its whites as Orvieto Classico *(Wine Tourism, 2023)* since the estate is located in one of the oldest areas of DOC Orvieto in the region, in itself very impressive, making it a good one to try the punchy whites. Among its white wines worth mentioning is an interesting clone of Grechetto, unusual because of its original characteristics and unlike others in the surrounding area. I would say try them all and enjoy every moment here - on any day apart from Sunday when it closes (FYI). There is room for 50 people max on their tour bookings, so book early and avoid disappointment. The Castello di Corbara winery is located at Localita' Corbara 7, 05018 Orvieto Terni.

- Palazzone: Here, for € 25+, you can enjoy a full and gloriously memorable itinerary that includes wine tasting and a guided walk around the vineyards. The estate and its surrounding landscapes are unquestionably charming, and you can choose a wine-tasting package that suits you best. Even a basic wine-tasting tour includes a full suite of wine tasting paired with local Umbria products. During the tasting activity, the company's representative will explain the history of Palazzone and Orvieto to visitors. For more info: https://palazzone.com/?lang=en

The history here itself is a masterclass and will have you lost in its richness - in 1969 the Dubini family bought the property Palazzone, constructed by Cardinal Teodorico at the request of Pope Boniface VIII, to provide a hostel for pilgrims on their way to Rome to celebrate the Jubilee (1300 A.D.) *(palazzone.com, 2023)* Today, it has been rebuilt in honour of the original architecture, as a boutique hotel with elegant suites and a winery to die for, just adjacent to Rocca Ripesena, with superb views of Orvieto.

Angelo Dubini planted 25 hectares of vines, and then in 1982, his two sons Giovanni and Lodovico made the first small vintage from these prestigious grapes. In 1988, they started constructing an entire winery to process all of their own grapes and also to begin commercial marketing of what is now the famed "Palazzone" wine of Umbria, regarded as one of the most significant labels in the region. *(palazzone.com, 2023)*

During a stay at the Palazzone winery, you can wander around the lush vineyards to your heart's content and admire the cultivation processes and the winery's appellation criteria for choosing unique grapes. The best thing about it here? The cellar, where large chestnut barrels are stored and a social media photo opportunity from heaven! The aromas of wines, stored in the barrels for maturation, give you an authentic Italian winery experience you always knew you needed. You can easily book a wine-tasting and Tour experience at Palazzone using their online service.

*Figure 57. Palazzone Winery*

As well as these impressive winery experiences of Umbria, the region also has hidden, affordable gems to offer; the Di Filippo in Trevi winery offers tours and tastings of their Sagrantino, Montefalco Rosso, and Grechetto wines starting at €15 per person. The experience includes a tour of the vineyards and cellar and a tasting of four wines paired with local cheeses and meats. This is a great spot for the humble, young, big tour groups who are looking for a fun day at the winery and don't want a 100 Euro lunch.

Another is Antonelli San Marco in Montefalco, which offers tours and tastings of the famed Sagrantino and Montefalco Rosso wines for €18 per person. The experience again includes a tour of vineyards and cellars and a tasting of more of the winery's best wines paired with local bread and olive oil. Italians can do nothing wrong with these ingredients; I'm not sure how they do it.

These are just a few examples of the many wineries in Umbria that offer amazing wine experiences and tastings for whatever your group's plans and budgets involve. Umbria will be a great region to spread your wine-loving wings! Currently, it boasts 13 DOC and two DOCG wine regions *(Somm TV, 2022)*, and hopefully, we have shown you plenty of varied locations to try some and all of these!

Finally, it is worth noting that consumers already recognise the white wines of Umbria in the Orvieto made from Grechetto and Trebbiano and the red wines of Montefalco made from Sangiovese and Sangrantino. However, that's changing slowly - Umbria has a lot of things one might find in Tuscany, but it is a wilder terrain, calmer and far less expensive. So, if you're ready to try a few different options, beat the crowds and get your feet on the Umbrian soils to try it all for yourself.

## Le Marche

Le Marche is our final stop in Central Italy - arguably one of the most underrated wine regions to visit in the whole of Italy. Therefore, I was especially keen to include it here and share some of the top wineries to visit, plus my additional recommendations and research for an outstanding wine trip with a more understated vibe. It is a phenomenally beautiful and relatively undiscovered area located between the Apennine Mountains and the Adriatic Sea; with such a diverse landscape, it is like rolling three other regions into one - hills, coastal areas, and charming mediaeval villages are all next door to one another.

Le Marche sits in between Rome and Florence, so is brilliantly located if you are coming long-haul by plane and looking to tick off one of the big Italian cities during your trip. It has the Adriatic to the east (cue a few beach days as well) and extends west towards the foothills of the Apennines and the Gran Sasso beyond. *(Decanter, 2019)*

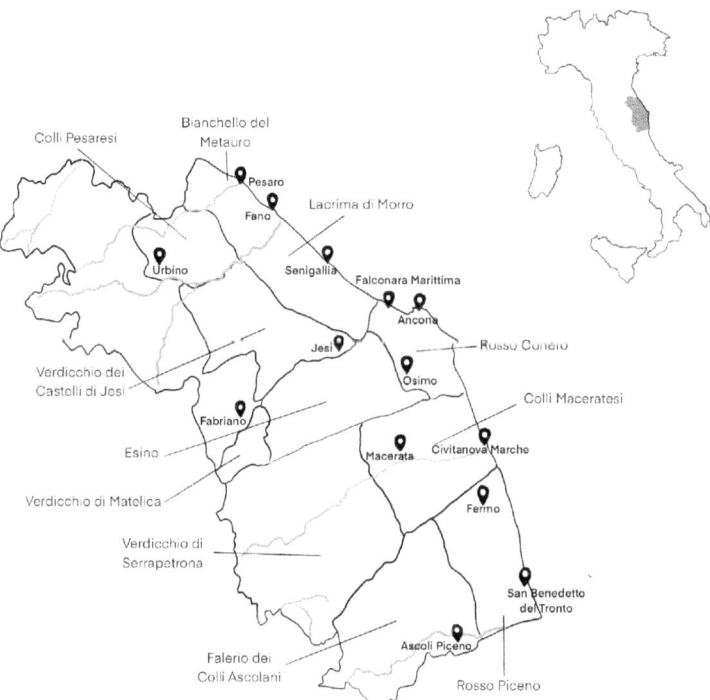

*Figure 58. Le Marche Regions*

Visiting a winery here is not about the glamour of luxury wine estates, nor will there be many on-site accommodation options - it is a rustic, Italian experience with plenty of charm and completely ideal vine-growing territory, so the quality of the wine itself is also exceptional. A 2019 well-publicised trip hosted by 'Marchet', the Marche Chamber of Commerce, proved that a substantial revolution is taking place *(Decanter, 2019)* and gave Umbria's reputation a rejig in terms of its wines, which was well overdue.

It is home to various indigenous and international grape varieties, including Verdicchio, Montepulciano, Sangiovese, and Pecorino. Verdicchio, in particular, is one of the region's most celebrated white wines, known for its crisp acidity, citrus notes, and excellent ageing potential. Now that Le Marche is coming out of the shadows of neighbouring Tuscany and the tourist-soaked regions, these flagship wines are starting to be truly celebrated. Today, two million hectolitres of wine are produced and have helped boost the overall reputation for the upfront quality of the area. *(Decanter, 2019)*

There is just as much excitement for red wine lovers in the region as for white - Rosso Conero and Rosso Piceno are two popular regional red wines, made primarily from Montepulciano grapes and often exhibiting rich flavours and soft tannins. Rosso Piceno, the latter, is a blend of Montepulciano and Sangiovese, creating a balanced red wine for all of you looking to try something a little easier on the palate.

Due to the understated nature of Le Marche, the region offers a vast option of small and boutique, family-run wineries that welcome visitors for tours and tastings and do so at a very reasonable price. These probably aren't the destinations to go with your most impressionable clientele for Michelin-starred private lunches, and instead, are perfect for the grounded, fun wine tour experience with a bunch of your closest friends. Of the wineries we love in this region, the below are just a few to try:

- Malacari is an estate winery and farm-based around Offagna and owned by the family after whom the winery has been named since the 16th century. Here, there is a great example of the Rosso Conero DOC to try and a riserva DOCG from 100% Montepulciano, produced organically from older vines with very little intervention. *(Decanter, 2019)* This estate has been making wine for centuries and is worth visiting. Hours and visits: Tuesday –Saturday, 15:30 to 19:30. There are several casual tasting options for those visiting without reservations, but it is advised to email ahead at info@malacari.it. Directions: This is only a 20-minute drive South East of Ancona

- Cantina Di Sante: The historic Di Sante organic farm at Carignano is set in the Colli Pesaresi area around Fano, and is everything good in the new winemaking scene. It is a leading educational base for food and wine nationally and internationally. It sees food and wine tourism as the new venture for tourism in the area it needs to be. The experience here is more a moment of quiet reflection, immersed in nature and works of art, taking in the land and the joys of biodynamic production. It has large open spaces, and the rich tufa soils of the estate support many varieties, including Bianchello, Sangiovese and Montepulciano wines – the full range, including olive oil and grappas, oil, grape juice and vinegar of our production can be found in their wine shop in Fano itself, accompanied by typical Marche products such as homemade bread, cured meats, cheeses, honey and jams. The times for the wine tastings are Mondays at 10.00/12.00 17.00/19.00, Wednesdays at 10.00/12.00 17.00/19.00 and Fridays at 10.00/12.00 17.00/19.00.

Booking is preferred, and a visit is by reservation only on Tuesday, Thursday, Saturday and Sunday. For bookings, you can call 0721885627 or email ahead at info@disantevini.it for a winery and olive grove tour. Directions: This is a further 10 minutes up the coast from Bruscia winery, where we visit next...

- Bruscia Vini is an excellent example of an Umbria family-run winery business where great care is taken in the production and end product. Le Marche grapes are grown across a 50-hectare estate in the hillsides around Constanzo *(Decanter, 2019)*. The principal white wine here is Bianchello, with Sangiovese for the red fans. Lesser known varieties include a white Incrocio Bruni and a small quantity of Lachryma produced here - this is the thin-skinned 'weeping' grape *(Decanter, 2019)* and no tears from anyone here, please.

A new cellar was built at Bruscia Vini in the past few years. It is super tech and the home of wine production. It would appeal to those with a (secret or otherwise) love of design, spanning over 800 square metres of impressive new design. The winery has the best machinery and technology required for modern-day winemaking. The winemakers are experienced and capable of finding the right balance between tradition and modernity for the wines.

Bruscia won many national and international awards for its wines. The winery gets its grapes locally from vineyards in San Costanzo. Bianchello, along with Malvasia and Incrocio Bruni, are the main grape for white wine. The region has great soil, sun exposure, and a perfect climate for vine cultivation.

At the winery, work is done with organic methods certified by the Soil and Health Authority. Since 2012, their wines have been labelled fully organic and now use the logo that ensures the product is officially BIO. Hours and visits: Open Monday – Friday, and it is best to email [info@brusciavini.it](info@brusciavini.it) to book and confirm arrival times. You will find Bruscia Vini at Strada Cerasa 11/A, San Costanzo, Marche, 61039 - a 40-minute north from Ancona up the stunning coastline - nothing to complain about this journey at all.

- Società Agricola Ciù Ciù: Along the same stunning coastline drive, but an hour and ten-minute drive South of Ancona towards San Benedetto del Tronto, is the vegan heaven that is Società Agricola Ciù Ciù winery. This is a certified organic family winery, founded in 1970 and celebrated for its astounding sensitivity to Italian cultural heritage and sustainability efforts. The estate is made up of 300 hectares of organic and biodynamic vines. Ciù Ciù Tenimenti Bartolomei as an empire has several sites all across Italy and represents a vegan wine heritage that spreads far beyond just Le Marche - more famous, large estates such as Feudo Luparello in Sicily; Villa Barcaroli in Abruzzo; Rocca Sinibalda in eastern Sabina, Lazio and; Maremma in Tuscany. *(ciuciutenimenti-it 2023)*

The Marche little jewel of the empire is Palazzo Mercolini-Tinelli, in Offida, the Ascoli Piceno area of Le Marche. Although small, the winery is certainly mighty: it offers visitors and wine buyers the full range of local white varietals, including Verdicchio, Pecorino and Passerina, and the very finest of the premium reds, including Montepulciano, Sangiovese, Barbera, Merlot and Cabernet. *( 2023)* No animal products are used during the process and roll on the shout-out for the commitment to veganism and biodynamic practices.

Note that the shop and tasting room are in Offida itself, so they are only a short trip away. Hours and visits: Advised to fill out the form online *(* with at least a week's notice for a wine tour. And you will find it an hour and ten-minute drive South of Ancona along the coast to San Benedetto del Tronto.

A visit to the Mount Conero wine estate area is a must for nature lovers. This protected natural area offers hiking trails with panoramic views of the Adriatic coast and the surrounding countryside and covers around 5,800 hectares. It is a haven for nature lovers and outdoor enthusiasts with well-maintained trails that wind through forests, rocky cliffs, and scenic viewpoints. Here, you will find some of the most beautiful beaches on the Adriatic coast, such as Spiaggia delle Due Sorelle and Spiaggia di San Michele.

All of the beauty in areas like Mount Conero and the charming wine scene we have covered together shows how Umbria delivers in its authenticity and unspoiled charm, making it an ideal destination for wine enthusiasts seeking unique experiences off the oversaturated wine track. Whether exploring the vineyards, savouring the wines, or immersing yourself in the region's history, Le Marche promises a memorable and enriching journey.

**Summary of Chapter 5**

In this Chapter, we have covered the breadth of Central Italy that can possibly be covered in one book. We explored the most famous powerhouse of Italian wine regions, Tuscany - and the wine varietals to find there as well as where to find them, namely Chianti, Brunello di Montalcino, Vino Nobile di Montepulciano and the Super Tuscans, blending Sangiovese with international grape varieties - such as Cabernet Sauvignon and Merlot.

Some of the big, commercial and incredibly well-known wineries we looked at together were Antinori, Frescobaldi and Castello Banfi, all offering world-renowned experiences and tours. If you choose a globally recognised winery of this kind, then you will find many options online for booking via a tour company or by going direct, so do your research and be reminded to find the best tour that suits you.

We then moved to Brunello di Montalcino wines, which are produced in the Montalcino area of Tuscany and are highly regarded for their quality and elegance. Brunello di Montalcino is considered one of Italy's most prestigious red wines, and we explored where in Tuscany it is best to find great wine tours and tastings of it. Lastly, in Tuscany, for those with longer and a budget to match, we looked at what a longer trip to the famous region could look like - a well-planned journey travelling in style right across Tuscany from the area of Val D'Orcia to the beaches of Viareggio possibly; then from Carrara's marble quarries to the buzz of the Mediterranean coastline.

Moving to neighbouring Umbria, in this chapter, I hope I successfully shared how, comparatively, the experiences at wineries will differ from the relatively flamboyant Tuscany. We then looked at where to find the region's notable white wines, such as Orvieto and Grechetto, and reds, such as Sagrantino di Montefalco. The Umbrian wines we looked at showcase a balance between tradition and innovation, reflecting the region's terroir. In this chapter, when looking at Umbria, I shared some suggested routes for a longer wine trail experience, like starting in Torgiano, 15 km from Perugia, continuing to Bevagna, Montefalco, and ending at Spoleto. All along this route, there are marvellous wine stopovers we explored, taking you through the most beautiful hills in Umbria and beyond.

Lastly, in Central Italy, we delved into Le Marche, one of the smallest and most under-rated wine regions to visit in the country... wait, maybe the world. We explored some of the region's small, family-run and understated beautiful wineries. I shared Wine tours here, which are a rustic Italian experience with plenty of charm and near-perfect indigenous and international wines, including Verdicchio, Montepulciano, Sangiovese, and Pecorino.

Now that Le Marche is coming out of the shadows of neighbouring Tuscany and the tourist-soaked regions nearby, I hope these flagship Le Marche wines are starting to be truly celebrated and enjoy the same esteem as the wider Central Italy wine region.

CHAPTER 6

# TOUR OF SOUTHERN ITALY'S WINE REGIONS

Italy's southern regions have varied cultures and flagship wine varieties but are all united by their passion for wine and unrivalled Italian hospitality. In covering Southern Italy for the sake of this chapter, we will also include the islands of Sicily and Sardinia, mainly to ensure there is no chance of these fabulous wine destinations being missed. However, the islands are separate from the Italian mainland, and you could write a whole book on the wine scene on each of these wonderful islands themselves.

With Southern Italy in mind, we evoke images of world-class beaches and seaside villas with vineyards, winery-owned hotels and rolling hills. Any true lover of Italian wine who loves to travel needs to look beyond some of the better-known, Northern and Central wine regions covered so far, to explore the fantastic regions of Italy's south, below Rome, in search of wine estates - particularly those with accommodation and offering the whole holiday package.

These less-visited Southern regions really evoke the most quintessentially Mediterranean aspects of Italian culture we love as holidaymakers, that have been garnered by thousands of years of occupation, from the Greeks and Byzantines to the Arabs and Bourbons. *(Decanter, 2020)*

*Figure 59. Magna Graecia*

I have chosen a selection of fabulous places to visit, drink and stay in four regions in Southern Italy - Campania, Puglia and the islands of Sardinia and Sicily - each with world-class wine and finely tuned Italian custom ready to welcome you with a warm *Salute*.

## Campania

Firstly to Campania, a wine region in Southern Italy that is known for its rich and complex red wines such as Taurasi and Aglianico del Taburno. Campania's historical winegrowing background dates back to the 12th Century BC, one of Italy's oldest wine regions.

As well as being known for its reds made from the above grapes, it is perhaps even more loved for its whites, such as Fiano di Avellino. Wineries in Campania are always open and welcoming to guests, and wineries are keen to share their wines and winemaking history with visitors. You will find many of the most famous of the region's wineries near Naples or Amalfi, as well as hundreds of others and attractions throughout other areas. Other wine areas in the Campania region include:

- Taurasi: Located in the Avellino province, Taurasi is a key wine region known for producing powerful Aglianico-based reds. The wines are known for their structure and ageing potential.

- Irpinia: The broader Irpinia region encompasses Taurasi and is known for its diverse grapes and wine styles, including Fiano, Greco, and Aglianico wines.

- Amalfi Coast: The picturesque Amalfi Coast is known not only as a dreamy holiday destination but also for its breathtaking landscapes and terraced vineyards. Wines from this region, often produced in small quantities, offer a taste of the coastal terroir.

- Sannio: The Sannio region produces a variety of wines, both red and white, with a focus on indigenous grape varieties. This region is known for its accessibility and the diversity of its wine offerings.

Due to the region's entire geographical position and the favourable climate of the South of Italy, wineries in Campania can be visited all year round - you won't really get a 'bad' month here, just maybe a bit of rain in the winter - which if you are from the UK, is nothing unusual. Wineries here have strong historical links to their wine, and vines are managed by respected and experienced winemakers *(Wine Tourism, 2023)* and many wineries in the area have underground cellars where the wines are aged in oak barrels for several years, paying homage to patience. Campania wineries will be quick to proudly share with you their great vineyard management, harvesting methods and cellar techniques. *(Wine Tourism, 2023)*

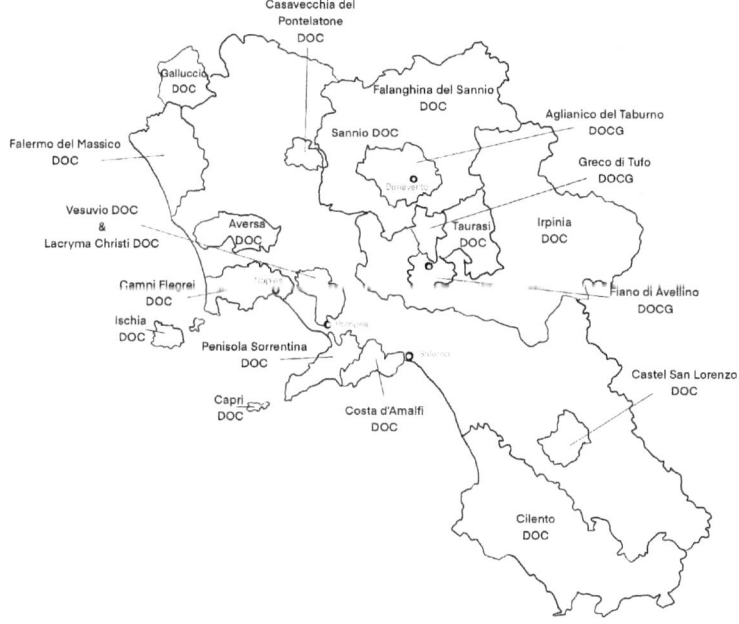

*Figure 60. Campania Region*

The most famous and popular indigenous red grape of the region is Aglianico, and perhaps the reason for booking your trip there, who knows? But if not, other grape varietals grown by wineries in Campania to an excellent standard, are:

- Fiano
- Greco
- Greco Nero
- Falanghina

Some of the larger, world-class wineries to consider visiting in Campania, before we branch out to the niche ones, include Feudi di San Gregorio, Mastroberardino, and Mustilli:

- Feudi di San Gregorio

Feudi di San Gregorio in Sorbo Serpico, Campania, has long been a haven of modernity in the rural hills of the Campanian hinterland. *(Decanter, 2020)* If coming from Naples airport to the Campania region, it is less than an hour's drive east, towards the upper peaks of the Apennines above Sorbo Serpico. With sweeping views of hills and vines, the winery's central buildings were designed by the Japanese architect Hikaru Mori in 2001. *(Decanter, 2020)* She brought an elegant aesthetic to an area best known for its rusticity but one which has been well-received and sensitively intertwined with the old. The graphic design of the late Massimo Vignelli complemented her directive and gave Feudi di San Gregorio an unmistakable look. *(Decanter, 2020)* The creative genius of designer Massimo Vignelli had been the visionary and helm of the winery's identity and designed all of its labels. Over the years, this collaboration with Vignelli has become synonymous with Feudi's brand identity - extending to the feel and design of the winery's interiors, stands when they exhibit worldwide, its publications and the famous packaging for FeudiStudi wines. *(Feudi.com, 2023)*

This means visitors can tour not only the cellars and vineyards but also get an almost art-gallery experience and a cultural day out - you can view decades' worth of its modern art installations, absorb the design story and interiors, and learn all about the low-impact approach the winery now practises. Winemaking is considered an art form at Feudi - one that is celebrated every day and how they target projects. The fresh and relatively new winery, which opened in 2004, revolves around wine-making but also around hospitality, providing the perfect backdrop for everything from a tasting for a small group to playing host to huge private business meetings and events for locals. You can also see the wine varietals all in their finery in the wine cellar in Sala Balthazar, an incredible space specifically designed for conviviality and tastings, which almost becomes a small theatre where wine is the star. *(Feudi.com, 2023)*

Finally, a meal in the award-winning panoramic restaurant, Marennà, is world-class here. Forget a few local cheeses to match your wine - here, the food is seriously high-end, and features Campanian ingredients, Neapolitan traditions and dishes that complement the estate's wines, from the three classic local DOCG wines – Fiano di Avellino, Greco di Tufo and Taurasi – as well as from more recent projects, like the sparkling Dubl wines from native grapes vinified in the style of Champagne. *(Feudi.com, 2023)* The wine selection extends beyond just the family's estates in Campania, Basilicata and Tuscany, to local producers renowned for their outstanding quality and respect for tradition. It has more than 250 labels, exceeding 2,000 bottles of wine in total and including rare vintages and shamelessly flashy special bottle sizes from Magnum to Balthazar. Huge emphasis is placed on tastings and vertical tastings, paired with dishes prepared by the Head chef. Contact details are as follows: https://www.feudi.it/ Address: Località Cerza Grossa, 83050 Sorbo Serpico Phone Number: +39 0825 986611

- Mastroberardino

Mastroberardino sits on the Via Manfredi 75-81 in Atripalda, Avellino and is an old family estate that has been in winemaking for three centuries. It is said that the original founder, Berardino, received the title of "Maestro" and founded his first winery in the XVII century in the heart of the Irpinia wine region *(Wine Tourism, 2023)* Then, the farm was officially registered in 1878 by the great-great-grandfather of the current owner, Professor Piero Mastroberardino, Cavalier Angelo. *(Wine Tourism, 2023)*

That's it for the history lesson, I promise. Still, it is to say that the Mastroberardino family to this day has always preserved and spread the values and significance of wines from Irpinia. Nowhere in Campania will you find the region's pride more evidently shared than at Mastroberardino - it holds dear a mission to protect, share and promote the winemaking traditions of the Campania region while acknowledging ecology and environment. *(Wine Tourism, 2023)*

It is also the largest producer of premium wines in Campania - as well as producing some of the best wines in the region, Mastroberardino is known for its contribution to the preservation of local ( or "autochthonous") varieties. *(Wine Tourism, 2023)* Antonio Mastroberardino is the grandfather of the current winemaker, Piero - so yes, the name came from somewhere - who is known for his effort to revitalise Campania's ancient and native grapes. He is credited with having saved and revived the Fiano, Greco and most famous of all, Aglianico, varietals after they were nearly wiped out by phylloxera in the 1930s. *(Wine Tourism, 2023)*

Antonio Mastroberardino was entrusted by the Italian government to restore ancient vineyards near the city of Pompeii, in a mission called the Villa dei Misteri. The main task was to recreate the vineyards, varieties, cultivation and production of wines, just as it had been done in the Roman era. *(Wine Tourism, 2023)* The first of these vintages from historical vineyards were released in 2001, to huge acclaim and something that has been well celebrated and linked to the winery's name ever since.

*Figure 61. Pompeii*

The ancient cellar at Mastroberardino deserves a special mention - its vaults were decorated with paintings by Raffaele De Rosa, and Maria Mikotzy, and the creations share tales of ancient associations, with the whole basement serving as an art gallery experience, with frescoed vaulted ceilings. *(Wine Tourism, 2023)* There is nowhere more surreal and artistic to enjoy your wine tasting than among nymphs and elegantly-painted women braiding into vines and dancing among barrels and barricades - at least now you know it's not that you've had one too many. Contact details https://mastroberardino.com/  Address: Mastroberardino Societa' Agricola, Via Manfredi 75/81. Atripalda  Phone number: +39 0825 614111  Email: pr@mastroberardino.com

- Mustilli

The famous Mustilli Ancestors moved to the ancient Samnium region of Campania in the mediaeval village of Sant'Agata de' Goti in the 16th century, in order to cultivate the lands of Benevento. *(Strade Bianche Wines, 2023)* Then, in the 1970s Leonardo and Marilì Mustilli re-established the family tradition of grapevine cultivation reintroducing Campania's most well-known varietals we have mentioned above, such as Greco, Aglianico and Falanghina, which at that time were close to extinction. *(Strade Bianche Wines, 2023)*

Leonardo Mustilli was impressed by the Falanghina varietal and in 1979, he bottled the first pure Falanghina wine in the world. *(Strade Bianche Wines, 2023)* Today his daughters run the hugely successful family business and winery - Paola is in charge of the commercial aspects, and Anna Chiara oversees the vineyards, winemaking and quality control. *(Strade Bianche Wines, 2023)*

This is a wine lovers' paradise if you want to see old traditions being honoured, and cellars dug into the tuff, 15 metres below the family palace *(Strade Bianche Wines, 2023)* Down here is also the wine bar where a simple, classic version of wine tastings take place. Palazzo Rainone is a historic residence that hosts visitors wanting to immerse themselves in the wider mediaeval village at the foot of Mount Taburno. *(Strade Bianche Wines, 2023)*

The Mustilli aura of a family-run company is evident everywhere on site - and it is an honour to see a winery so dedicated to safeguarding local production. Beyond that, it spreads a cultural message of good food and a quality of life across all their communications. Staying true to it, the Mustilli family host and organise events dedicated to the world of art, music and culture that take place in the courtyard or ancient cellars or the historic residence and welcome the local community to share in their zest for wine-making and Italian dolce vita. *(Strade Bianche Wines, 2023)*

Next, I want to share all things organic and celebrate a lesser-known Campania winery - I Cacciagalli in Teano, a perfect winery for lovers of natural, biodynamic and organic wines in the Italian wine industry. The wine estate is in the province of Caserta (north-west of Naples) and offers a stylish yet very affordable location to stay *(Decanter, 2020)* with accommodation to suit not only trendy wine groups (may or may not be you) but the whole family. The look of the winery is sparse but well-designed (see below for our take on it), with wood and pale natural tones setting the scene of a simple and chic world of wine.

The wines at I Cacciagalli Teano are made in large, old-fashioned clay amphorae. When you think of wine in ancient times, you probably picture a large amphora as the traditional item used. It is like going back in time - the amphora was used centuries ago to transport liquids (including wine) and for wine-making. Shaped like a vase, with two ears as handles, the large clay amphora is coming back in wineries worldwide. *(aveine.fr, 2021)* When winegrowers began to notice the perfect characteristics of terracotta for winemaking, there was no looking back, and it became central once again to the winemaking process.

Owner of I Caccaiagalli Mario Basco and his young family live on the property and look after the guests personally *(Decanter, 2020)*. It is quite possibly the most wonderful version of an Airbnb experience as you could expect to find - surrounded by countryside and vineyards. They grow the local varieties of this post-volcanic area, including Aglianico, Falanghina, Fiano and Piedirosso. The restaurant's ingredients are sourced from local organic producers, and meals are served in an attractive dining room.

This is a beautiful part of the Italian countryside to explore further, with the above accommodation as your base. The majestic Reggio di Caserta – a royal palace designed by Vanvitelli for the House of Bourbon and based on Versailles – is a short distance away. *(Decanter, 2020)* Combining the influences of Versailles, Rome, and Tuscany, the Caserta 'Royal Palace and Park' is a historical hotspot to explore on your doorstep.

Caserta is considered a triumph of Italian Baroque and vastly ahead of its time. *(Visit World Heritage, 2023)* The site expands across 11 acres, with pools and fountains, and cascades through a 'telescope effect' and provides everything you need (apart from the wine, which you can head home for later) for a delightful cultural day out nearby.

If I Caccaiagalli doesn't quite suit the needs of your wine tour group, then other wineries in the region which also have accommodation on-site include the below and have complete details about prices and booking options on their websites directly:

- Contea De' Altavilla: https://www.conteadealtavilla.com/

- Villa Raiano: https://www.villaraiano.com/en/

- Le Masciare: https://www.lemasciare.com/en/the-farmhouse/

- Cantina Del Barone: https://www.winetourism.com/experience/wine-tasting-and-tour-at-cantina-del-barone/

My other two further important winery recommendations in the Campania region, in the interest of, unfortunately, not being able to sweep the whole region for its pizza + wine tastings, are below:

- D'Antiche Terre

D'Antiche Terre has various vineyards spread across the region, including Tuff, Saint Pauline, Prato Principato Ultra, Pratola Serra, Pietradefusi, Montefusco, Manocalzati and Torre le Nocelle. *(Wine Tourism, 2023)* So it is very likely you have been in their winemaking environment and perhaps not even have known it. The rolling hills of the vineyards in the D'Antiche Terre Winery make it effectively one of the area's main epicentres of wine production, where ancient traditions meet modern winemaking techniques.

The large wine-making spaces on the main winery have been renovated to accommodate more modern tastes and with a conscious effort to engage the new wine tourism in the region. *(Wine Tourism, 2023)* This perfect blend of old and new is evident in every aspect, from the vine to the bottles. For 15 €, you can enjoy a perfect 3-hour package of wine tasting and a tour, trying each of their three finest quality three DOCG wines, Fiano di Avelino, Greco di Tefo and Taurasi. The address is Via Variante Est N. 74,

Manocalzati, 83030, Italy and all other details accessible on the website www.danticheterre.it

- Le Vigne Di Raito

Le Vigne Di Raito winery is another winery in Campania I want to share. The terraced vineyards cover an area of about two hectares and are cultivated with a typical Amalfi Coast method that involves bordering with macere. *(Wine Tourism, 2023)* Several tour companies offer experiences among these vineyards, from a simple picnic and wine tasting in the vines to a whole experience day with paired dinner or cooking courses. These are available through Wine Tourism online, other wine tour agents, and directly via the winery themselves at https://www.levignediraito.com/ Address: Via San Vito, 9 Raito, Vietri Sul Mare 84019.

This is a haven for plant and nature lovers and an impressive site for wine production. Mediterranean plants like oaks, olive trees, pomegranates and strawberry trees are everywhere, and farm buildings are being renovated to bring it to the present day. Most of the work is done by hand, and fertilisers or chemicals are not used. Hence, Le Vigne Di Raito has been certified 'biodynamic' for its sustainable and organic methods. *(Wine Tourism, 2023)*

The Aglianico and Piedrosso grapes are the main ones that grow here and are used to make the Costa d'Amalfi DOC wines. Without the chemicals and additives, the wines retain a natural, fruity flavour and have a strong taste and intense aroma. The wines are of high quality and rightly reflect the true nature of their terroir and hard graft by hand in the winemaking and bottling processes.

As we leave Campania, I hope you get to see the highlights of the red wines we have covered, such as Aglianico-based wines from Taurasi and Irpinia and the exceptional whites in the form of Fiano di Avellino and Greco di Tufo. Campania's rich history and wine culture make it a great region to visit, and the region's cuisine beautifully complements Campania's wines. Visiting Campania allows one to explore vineyards, cellars, and historic sites.

Cities like Naples offer a vibrant atmosphere and a cultural highlight, while the Amalfi Coast offers stunning coastal beauty. Wine-tasting tours across the region allow you to discover the best of both and the diverse wines of the region with the passionate people who craft them.

## Puglia

Moving now to Puglia, a wine region next door in southeastern Italy that is known for its bold and flavourful red wines, such as Primitivo and Negroamaro.

Many wineries in the area have cellars where the wines are aged in oak barrels or bottles for several years, just waiting for you on your wine trip of a lifetime to choose them for drinking there and then or to send home by the crateload. As we said earlier in the book, Puglia can be a great option in choosing value for quality, known for producing wines with excellent value for their standard. The region's wines often provide a balance between price and taste, making them accessible to lots of varied wine groups.

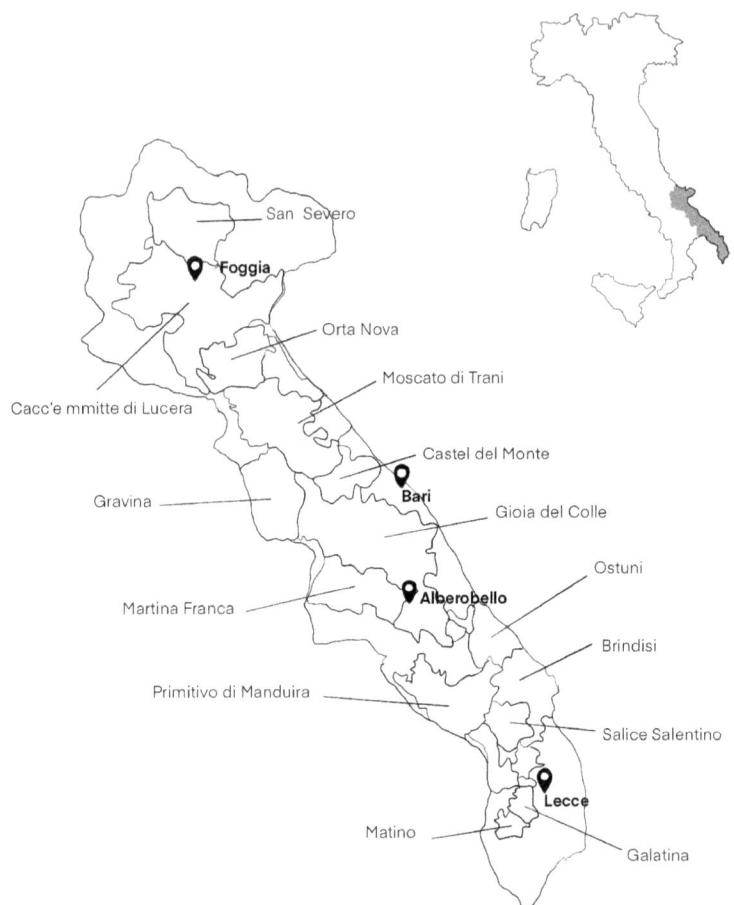

*Figure 62. Puglia Region*

Puglia has many indigenous grape varieties, including Primitivo, Negroamaro, and Fiano. These grapes are well-suited to the region's climate and terrain, leading to cost-effective cultivation and production - which means the region can afford to produce a lot of them! You can find everything from easy-drinking table wines to more complex and aged options, which means there is something for everyone in Puglia to find wines that fit their preferences and budgets.

The difference is that, unlike some other high-profile wine regions, Puglia's wines often come from smaller, family-run wineries with lower marketing and branding expenses, contributing to more affordable prices. Winning for all involved.

As Puglia's wine tourism industry grows, many wineries offer affordable tours and tastings, allowing visitors to sample and learn about the region's wines without breaking the bank. If Primitivo is your favourite wine grape, so famed in this region, then Manduria in Puglia is a great place to find it.

Indeed, in this area of sun-baked flat vineyards, you will find outstanding wineries among a landscape otherwise filled with rolling fields, Baroque churches, centennial olive trees and old watchtowers. Manduria is 35km from Taranto and 50km from Brindisi, on Italy's Puglian 'heel' *(Decanter, 2020)* and makes an excellent base from which to explore both coasts and many a winery.

*Figure 63. Vinilia Resort*

Vinilia Wine Resort, for example, is one excellent Primitivo winery based here, from an early 20th-century stone castle. The beautiful villa has been converted into an entire resort of sorts (there's a rhyme for free) with a hotel and spa, options for events, and a Michelin-starred restaurant, Casamatta, that features modern and stunning Puglian cooking. Vinilia Wine Resort was born from an ancient mansion dating back to the early '900 century and built by the aristocratic family Schiavone of Manduria. *(Vinilia resort, 2023)* It appears like a manor house to a modern visitor, but not in an intimidating way, but rather in a 'get me in that pool' kind of way. It has original towers and turrets, features decorative styles of the past, and a main building that resembles a small medieval castle. Indeed, if you were looking to get married in Puglia, you couldn't go far wrong here.

The Lacaita and Parisi Families later purchased the property, which was completely restored, saving it from the abandonment it would have doubtlessly faced otherwise. A beautiful internal staircase spreads over three floors, restoring the original charm and bringing new life to the building.

While the resort's vineyards are situated a few kilometres away, the accommodation itself is a rest day worth spending no more than 10 feet from the pool anyway - it can be booked directly via the Vinilia Resort website or mainstream booking agents websites like booking.com and alike. The nearby town of Manduria, where the vineyards are, is well worth visiting and has an interesting wine museum dedicated to the culture of its native grape, Primitivo. There are fabulous beaches nearby, villages, and local wineries to explore, so this is more a space to base yourself if wine touring is one of many relaxing holiday pursuits during your stay.

Some other wineries to consider visiting in Puglia if you want to be on-site and with a full glass of wine at all times include Cantine Due Palme, located in Cellino San Marco, in the heart of the Salento region of Puglia. It is one of the largest and most renowned wineries in Southern Italy, known for producing quality wines - and one not to miss if you've come to Puglia for the wine.

It offers guided tours of the winery and vineyards, providing insights into winemaking techniques and the region's viticulture while giving your visit a personalised feel. If you are the one with a notepad at these things, at Cantine Due Palme, you will learn everything from the history of the area, the grape varieties cultivated, and the winemaking process from vine to bottle. It is a great place to see those stages of winemaking we visited earlier in the book.

During your visit, you'll also have the opportunity to taste various wines - let's get to the important bit after all. Varieties like Primitivo and Negroamaro will be at the top of the list, as well as reds, including a characterful wine made from Negroamaro grapes: Canonico Negroamaro Salento IGP, which is ruby red with light purple reflections, and ripe plums and sour cherry.

It is a really well-balanced wine with a pleasant palate and a long and consistent finish *(Catineduepalma.wine, 2023)* - one to try at this winery in particular. They also do four cracking whites here, including a Bagnara Fiano Salento and a Passo a due Bianco Salentino - all a snip of a cost at €10 each.

Cantine Due Palme offers a picnic experience alongside wine tastings with snackable lunch food pairings such as local cheeses, cured meats, and olive oil. Even better, they offer a package experience to see the vineyards and tour the local area by bike - both available as well as a normal wine tasting experience, for very reasonable costs between € 35 - € 40 per person bookable on the website www.cantineduepalma.wine

Another winery it would be a crime to oversee while in Puglia is Fatalone - a small, passionate estate rooted in the 19th century and run by a team committed to farming organically. Their Fatalone Primitivo Gioia del Colle 2021 is a flagship wine that is a fine example of an organic Primitivo to try in the region if you don't get to any others - it has a pronounced and complex profile of plum, prune, tobacco and sweet spice among other complex flavours. *(Noble Green Wines, 2023)*

The experts here will tell you their pride wine bottling is best suited to lamb dishes, particularly in North African styles, or veggie recipes like roast aubergine parmigiana. But I would say to you it's pretty great with everything on this theme, and only get the tagine out if the mood arises and you have hours of cooking time to spare. The farmhouses Masseria Maiana, Don Nicoletta and Messere Andrea have belonged to the family for centuries, while others have been acquired more recently. The empire has wine estates and the Wine Hotel Villa Donna Lisa, located in a park's ancestral building with 24 spacious rooms, of which 2 are suites. The hotel also features a bar, guest parking, and a beautiful swimming pool. It is located at Via Senatore Leone de Castris – via Marangi, 73015 Salice Salentino.

The experiences available for tours of the wines here are exciting yet still very reasonably priced - ranging from € 6 up to €40, you can either enjoy a simple classic tour, the 'Great Tradition version' for €25, or the full experience at the top end you can enjoy Guided tour to the historical offices, wine cellar and Museum 'Piero e

Salvatore Leone de Castris' followed by a selection of local small sharing plates paired with three wines.

You will see the whole process from the arrival of the grapes at the winery to the bottling system; this is a rare insight to get first-hand. Don't worry. There is plenty of time to buy the products at ' Il Bottegone Leone de Castris' near the winery. Please check the wines data sheets on www.leonedecastris.com on the 'wines' tab for up-to-date information. The full address is Via Senatore De Castris, 73015 Salice Salentino, and you can book directly on the website in advance.

If you're looking for another equally affordable group wine experience in the region, then it's time for a shout-out to Cantine Lorusso in Martina Franca, which offers tours and tastings of their Primitivo, Negroamaro, and Bianco d'Alessano wines at approx €15 per person. The experience includes a tour of the vineyards and cellar and a tasting of three wines paired with local cheeses and meats.

This is a simple but fun and cost-effective way to enjoy a day of wine and is undoubtedly a go-to if you're a young group and happy with lower-key food pairings.

If that's the case, Cantina Albea in Castel del Monte also offers tours and tastings of their Nero di Troia, Primitivo, and Aglianico wines starting at €10 per person. The experience includes a tour of the vineyards and cellar and a tasting of three wines paired with local snacks - nothing wrong with a great day for € 10 in my book!

Moving to the islands… because it's always time for a boat ride and the best European beaches, right?

## Sardinia

Now, because they can't be called 'Southern Italy' in all accuracy, let's dive over to Sardinia and taste the wines there, followed by the other Italian island of Sicily to do the Southern Italian islands justice in all their wine-glory rights.

Wine tasting in Sardinia should always start in the North if you can, where the whole Gallura region is famous for its exotic and flavourful wine grapes. It is a great place to start on the island. Vermentino is one of the most popular native varietals of grapes in Sardinia, which is grown exceptionally well right across this area. As a lesson refresher, these are the light-skinned wine grapes that give a distinct fruity aroma and an exotic taste and come in the form of renowned Vermentino di Gallura DOCG, the fragrant Moscato di Sardegna and the lesser known Nebbiolo and Nastarrè here. *(Deliciously Italy, 2022)*

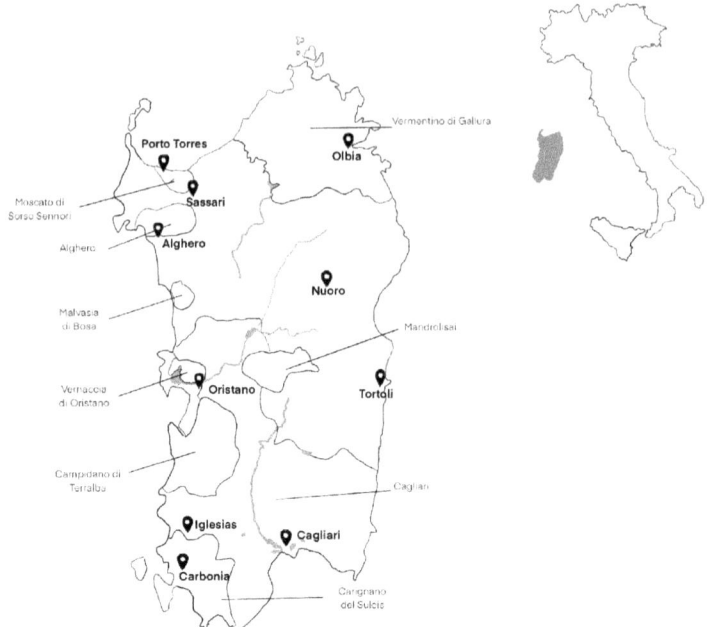

*Figure 64. Sardinia Region*

For wine lovers, the Gallura hinterland offers the island's drawcard. There is a route of sorts which can be explored to take in the best of this region, starting with the small agricultural centres of Tempo Pausania (Cantina Gallura), which surround Mount Limbara and stand out for their exceptional wines - and while here, Rena Bianca; one of the most beautiful beaches in the Mediterranean directly accessible from the town. *(Deliciously Italy, 2022)* You could venture inland to Luras, a characteristic village known for its white Vermentino di Gallura DOCG, the most exclusive production of the region's famous label. And finally, don't miss a visit to the wine cellars of the two small wine towns of Berchidda and Monti.

But first, my favourite recommendation in the North is the Capichera Winery in Gallura, a perfect place to experience pure Vermentino wine produced to perfection. In the late 1970s, the Ragnedda family decided to get the best out of Vermentino and sowed the nearby vineyards. Located in Arzachena amongst the gorgeous granite rock scenery of Gallura, the winery has mastered the art of producing pure Vermentino wine with a more refined ageing process, and the wine stays in wooden barrels until it is permanently fermented.

A range of tastings are proposed on-site here, typically from May to October, and the setting in the fine weather months is next to the beautiful country house among myrtle bushes and ancient oak trees. *(Deliciously Italy, 2022)* Three different options for wine tours are available here:

- The classic, lasting 90 to 120 minutes, is a tour of the estate in one of the Capichera Golfcarts - we are sold immediately, and who let us loose on one of these? It includes tasting a selection of traditional foods to accompany each label. For groups of more than 10 people, the tour is done on foot instead, so be sure to keep the group size down if you're in for the wheels.

- Superior is customised wine tasting combined with a rustic lunch, a genuine first-hand experience of the grape harvest, cooking classes, and trekking or bike tours of the vineyard. The price and duration depend on the elements involved picked from these.

- Cultural begins with a guided tour of an archaeological site located in a nearby historic vineyard, followed by a golf cart tour of the main Capichera estate. The wine tasting features two of the best Capichera wine bottlings and is guided by a knowledgeable sommelier. The entire experience lasts 4 hours and includes all entrance costs and transport for a maximum of four people to reach the archaeological sites. Lunch can also be included on request. *(Deliciously Italy, 2022)*

Cantina Li Duni, near Badesi in Olbia-Tempio in the North, has historic vines which grow freely and fiercely on the sandy ground just a stone's throw from the Asinara Gulf. As the relentless sun and unwavering winds continue to shape the island of Sardinia, Badesi vines remain some of the most significant benefactors in this Mediterranean paradise. Yes, the grapes of Cantina Li Duni have remained despite the nearby waters that have transformed this part of the Mediterranean into a traditional wine region.

Cantina Li Duni invites visitors to explore the wine cellars, where you can feel the care taken to produce such fine wines. Wine tasting ranks as one of the best things to do in Badesi, but the produce is pretty unique, too, and Sardinian wines like these are famous worldwide. Returning to the roots of wine-making in this region, visitors learn how these vineyards were integral to community life throughout history. Contact the winery by phone numbers +39 079 914 4480 / +39 388 426 3825 or an email via the online form at www.cantinaliduni.it/en/

Colline del Vento is a beautiful winery and one of the most notable activities in Villasimius on the island's Eastern side. Founded in 2006, the surrounding vineyard has belonged to the family for over a century, and wine-making was common here.

In fact, Colline del Vento features five acres of organic grapes, and the ocean view is nothing less than breathtaking. A father and son duo takes care of the grapevines here and has worked hard to perfect this ancient tradition and produce two different wines - Entu and Brennas.

According to the owner, the wind and sea play a large part in the blend of wine at Colline del Vento. After all, the family has always respected the principles of their ancestors and how their founders once cultivated the same land, and who am I to argue about wind direction? These conditions also make this the perfect place to relax, and there is very little to worry about with a wine glass in hand here.

Let's also cover the authentic delights of island life in Sardinia - every year in May, life tastes seriously good at the Porto Cervo Wine Festival. In the middle week of May, the Costa Smeralda celebrates this feel-good festival, featuring the best Sardinian and Italian winemakers. The wine-tasting event lasts for three days. It is held at the Cervo Conference Center and stretches down Porto Cervo's Piazzetta, roughly 4 kilometres north of Cala di Volpe. *(Decanter, 2020)*

If you time a wine trip perfectly to coincide with this, then you have a week of Italian wine tastings, lectures by nutritionists and representatives of the island, the Fashion Wine Walk, and gourmet dinner options at one of the most prestigious hotels in the area; Hotel Cervo, Pitrizza or Cala di Volpe. Tickets cost around €50 per person and include admission to the Conference Center, the tasting of various producer wines and admission to the festival. *(Decanter, 2020)*

Cantina li Seddi is a family-owned winery in the heart of the Gallura region, known for its beautiful landscapes and equally outstanding production of Vermentino wines. What can you expect when visiting Cantina Li Seddi for a wine-tasting experience? A guided tour of their vineyards and cellar, providing insights into the winemaking process and the characteristics of Vermentino grapes, as well as the unique terroir of Gallura and how it contributes to the flavour profile of the wines. After the tour, you'll have the opportunity to taste a selection of Cantina Li Seddi's Vermentino wines, from light and floral to more complex and mineral-driven.

In addition to wine, Cantina Li Seddi does local products like olive oil and other Sardinian specialities very well. These are excellent souvenirs or gifts to take home! As a family-run winery, Cantina Li Seddi may be able to offer a more personalised and intimate experience compared to larger commercial wineries. This can deepen your connection to the winemaking process and the people behind the wines. Contact Cantina Li Seddi in advance to ensure the booking of their tour and tasting sessions. Booking a reservation allows the winery to provide the best possible experience and timings that work for all. More info at https://www.cantinaliseddi.it/

Seek out these other winemakers in the north of the island:

- Tenuta Soletta, Vigne Deriu, Codrongianos (https://www.tenutesoletta.com/)

- Cantina Pedres, Olbia (https://www.cantinapedres.it/?lang=en)

- Gabriele Palmas, Sassari (https://www.gabrielepalmas.it/)

- Tenuta Dettori, Sennori (https://www.tenutedettori.it/en/)

*(Decanter, 2022)*

Gabriele Palmas is a chance to see the West of the island and a well-established quality vineyard with a winery that has become well-known in the global market. *(Wine Tourism, 2023)* The modest 15-hectare facility grows Vermentino and Cannonau, as well as Cabernet Sauvignon and Syrah, and was established in 2008.

This winery has received community recognition for producing outstanding Vermentino, red vintages of 1996, the 2016 Cabernet Riserva, and the 2016 Syrah, which have all won local awards. For €15, you can enjoy a short tour of the cellars and see the wines up close and personal, then try three of the wines from Cantine Gabriele Palmas while hearing how each bottle is produced. The address is 07100, Sassari, and you can either book directly at the Gabriele Palmas website or on www.winetourism.com

There is, of course, plenty to explore on the rest of the island - in addition to Vermentino and Cannonau, you'll have the chance to taste other indigenous grape varieties such as Carignano, Monica, and Nuragus across many wineries in other parts of the island, and each variety contributes to the diverse array of Sardinian wine.

For example, travelling to the very South near Cagliari, the capital of Sardinia, offers a mix of urban and rural wineries to try. Here, my tip is to visit wineries that produce a range of wines, from whites to reds and everything in between - literally; there are incredible rosé wines, orange wines, amber, sparkling and sweet with a rainbow of different grapes to try. A great place to do this is the Mulleri estate at Modolo.

Or even venture further down to the Southeasternmost tip to Colline Del Vento winery, where the owners, Mario and Gianluca, will welcome you to try their organic red and white wines and liquors accompanied by Sardinian treats. Here, you share a meal and wine with the owners as you would at a family dinner, and we loved it more than some of our own family gatherings, don't tell. Wine Tasting and activities at Colline del Vento can be booked directly online or also available at www.winetourism.com

*Figure 65. Sardinia DOCG Map*

Wine touring in Sardinia goes hand in hand with its rich culinary heritage, so enjoy the unique food and wine pairings that genuinely allow you to experience the link between Sardinian wines and local dishes. Sardinia's landscapes range from coastal vistas to rolling hills and rugged mountains, so the beauty of the island's natural surroundings won't make it hard to add to the charm of your wine tour if it covers distances in between.

Depending on the time of year, you might have the opportunity to attend wine festivals and events celebrating Sardinia's wines. As mentioned in the introductory chapters, I have often found myself at an impromptu Sardinian festival that I didn't know I'd been invited to, with a lively atmosphere for tasting and learning about the region's wines.

## Sicily

Hopping over to Sicily, our next stop is the famous island located off the southern coast of Italy, which in the wine world is known for its diverse range of wines, from crisp and refreshing whites to rich and complex reds. Sicily is known as an island at the crossroads of Mediterranean cultures and resonates with history enthusiasts and travellers seeking natural beauty. Sicily's location made it a coveted territory for various empires over the centuries, and as a result, the island boasts an amalgamation of cultures, cuisine, and traditions. Sicily's food and wine scene is a testament to this multicultural history, blending flavours from Arab, Greek, and Italian traditions. Don't miss getting your fix of arancini (rice balls), cannoli (sweet pastry), and fresh seafood while on the island.

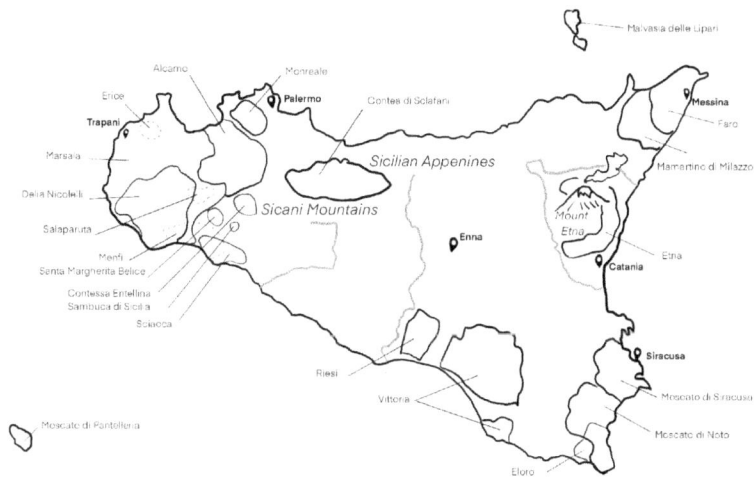

*Figure 66. Sicily Region*

Slipping into Sicily's wine world isn't difficult - it is home to renowned wine regions, including Marsala, and Etna, and famed for the Nero d'Avola grape. Most head for the Volcanic wineries of Mount Etna, which is more than just a volcano - it's a winemaker's paradise. Europe's tallest active volcano, Mount Etna, is also a UNESCO World Heritage Site. It offers opportunities for hiking, skiing (in winter), and exploring lunar-like landscapes for those to whom that appeals. For wine lovers, the fertile volcanic soils and high-altitude vineyards have been producing delicious wines for thousands of years, and it's the go-to wine destination on the island and an excellent place for exploring wine territory.

The history of winemaking on Mount Etna goes back to Ancient Greeks, Benedictine monks and even the Romans, who have all left their mark on Mount Etna's winemaking traditions.

If you have a secret or openly shameless love of history, then Mount Etna is for you. Modern winemakers are returning to traditional techniques used by their forefathers for some of the most exciting wines you could wish for in Italy. The volcanic vino terroir is one of the main reasons why the wines from this region are so unique and different. The volcanic soils are rich in minerals and nutrients, producing grapes with a distinct flavour. The high-altitude vineyards with cool temperatures (it's all relative; you will still have lovely warm days here) and a long growing season add to the grapes' complexity, resulting in rich wines in both flavour and acidity.

Red, white or rosé, Mount Etna has it all. The region's most famous wines are the reds made from the Nerello Mascalese grape, as mentioned in Chapter 1, but it's certainly not only a red-lover's terrain. White wines made from the Carricante grape are common in the area too - high in acidity with flavours of lemon, green apple and mineral notes, and plenty well worth getting into volcanic territory for.

Many excellent wineries on Mount Etna produce high-quality wines. Here are just a few that are worth checking out:

- Tenuta delle Terre Nere - This winery in Randazzo is known for its exceptional red wines made from the famous Nerello Mascalese grape mentioned above. On some level, it is a potential criminal to come to Scility and not try one of these reds, but your call, of course. The winery has vineyards in several different areas of Mount Etna, meaning you can be flexible as to when and where you do it based on your routine, and also meaning the winemakers produce wines that showcase the unique terroir of each different area of volcanic soil. For more info, check out their website at: https://www.tenutaterrenere.com/

- Benanti Winery - Benanti is one of the oldest wineries on Mount Etna and is known for its commitment to traditional winemaking - cue the history enthusiasts again. The winery produces a range of wines, including reds, whites and rosés, all made from grapes grown on the slopes of Mount Etna. Here is one to celebrate ancient traditions and history in front of your eyes. For more info, contact Benanti through their website: https://www.benanti.it/en/

- Graci - Graci is a charming, family-owned winery located in the town of Passopisciaro. The winery produces a range of wines, including reds again from the Nerello Mascalese grape and whites made from Carricante. The winery is known for its commitment to organic farming and sustainable winemaking practices and is huge for the feel-good factor. For more info, contact them at +39 348 701 6773.

These are just a few of the many excellent wineries on Mount Etna that are worth a visit and, depending on what you want and the group size & tastes, give you a few different options. Winemaking on Mount Etna is undoubtedly a traditional affair. Hand-harvesting, sorting, and organic or biodynamic farming are all standard practices in the region, and it is a real chance to see the process in its most organic form.

Large oak barrels or concrete tanks are used for ageing, allowing the wines to develop slowly and naturally, and you will be hard-pushed to find a winery that doesn't over-deliver on all aspects of tasting and friendly tour guide etiquette.

With their focus on traditional winemaking techniques and a commitment to sustainability, the producers of Mount Etna are creating some of the most exciting and dynamic wines in Italy.

So, pour yourself a glass of volcanic vino and toast to the gems of Sicily's wine world.

The Marsala wine region is located in the Western part of Sicily, Italy, near the town of Marsala. It is renowned for producing the fortified wine that shares its name and is a blend of indigenous and international grape varieties, including Grillo, Catarratto, Inzolia, and Damaschino. The wine gains its unique character through a process that involves fortification with grape spirits and ageing in oak casks - so you know we want to see that first-hand.

Marsala wine has a rich history dating back to the late 18th century when English trader John Woodhouse is credited with introducing fortified wine production techniques to the region. Since then, Marsala has become internationally recognised and enjoyed as a versatile wine for cooking and sipping. The main styles include Fine, Superiore, Vergine, and Riserva.

The production of Marsala involves a solera-style ageing system, where younger wines are blended with older ones over time to achieve consistency and complexity. The wine is aged in oak barrels, and its finished product is something to savour - plus is often a key ingredient in various Italian culinary dishes, especially sauces, risottos, and desserts. When visiting the Marsala wine region, you can explore local wineries and cellars that offer tours and tastings, showing you all stages of this unique process and distinct wine varietals. These visits provide insights into the production process of Marsala wine and allow you to sample the different styles.

Cantine Aperte, or "Open Cellars," is an annual wine event in Sicily where wineries open their doors to the public. It's a wonderful opportunity to visit Marsala wineries in particular (although others open their doors too), taste their wines, and immerse yourself in the local wine culture.

Cantine Barbera in Marsala is one of these, which year-round opens its doors and offers tours and tastings of its Marsala wines starting at €15 per person. The experience includes a winery and barrel cellar tour and a tasting of three different Marsala wines paired with local pastries and desserts. Find out more at https://www.cantinebarbera.it/en/sicily-menfi-wine-tasting.html

Cantine Florio, also in Marsala, does the same, with tours and tastings of their fortified wines also starting at €15 per person. The experience includes a tour of the historic cellars, as well as a tasting of three wines paired with local snacks. For more info, contact them at https://www.duca.it/florio/

As if heaven didn't already exist on the island of Sicily itself, there is even more to see on the volcanic Aeolian islands that belong to Sicily - one of which is the tiny island of Salina *(Decanter, 2020)*. Here you will find a few precious wineries, such as Capofaro, owned and run by the Tasca d'Almerita family, who have long been considered royalty of Sicilian winemaking. Its headquarters are in the Sicilian heartlands of Regaleali on the island, but in recent years, the wine estates have expanded to Salina. *(Decanter, 2020)* Capofaro is the perfect, idyllic and peaceful getaway for wine lovers... in fact, actual lovers, if we are honest. It comprises 27 rooms, each with its own entrance and built among the vineyards where the grapes for the delicious dessert wine, Malvasia delle Lipari, are grown in front of your eyes. You can reserve your visit directly through reservation.capofaromalvasiaresort@icastelli.net

The Capofaro estate overlooks the sea, so unlike many hilly vineyard regions of Italy, the beaches are nearby (if not somewhat volcanic), and the resort has a swimming pool. This is more of an all-in-one holiday than just a winery experience, and you would want at least a few days to maximise the beauty of the place and use all your bath towels, let's face it.

The on-site restaurant buzzes like a trendy hotel eatery and offers the best Mediterranean dishes, such as fresh seafood and salads, dashed with capers, olives and herbs. *(Decanter, 2020)* The chef, Ludovico De Vivo (as of 2023), creates his recipes from Sicilian influence, including aristocratic food from the region's golden age - so don't expect low-key food here.

For those who want to learn how to cook, a lovely additional activity here is cooking classes available on request, as are day trips to the other islands and tours of Salina, as well as a highly recommended yoga retreat.

Moving the spotlight south of the main island, let's take a closer look at Vittoria, a small town in the south-east of Sicily known for its unique red wine made from the Frappato grape. The Frappato Vittoria D.O.C. wine is made from 100% Frappato grapes and is a rare and exclusive variety cultivated only on these few hectares in the whole of Sicily in the red sands of Vittoria. *(Planeta.it, 2023)*

It is an aromatic red wine which, after de-stalking the grapes, is followed by 7 days on the skins and a soft pressing with the vertical press and fermentation in stainless steel vats. The versatility of this Sicilian Claret makes it perfect to pair with the type of 'everyday' Italian dishes that make all mouths water, like spaghetti Bolognese and lasagne. *(Planeta.it, 2023)*

*Figure 67. Main Regions in Sicily*

Although we have ticked off the most well-known areas of the island, there are many other boltholes of outstanding wine tasting that you can look out for, such as:

Menfi: A coastal region which produces wines with a Mediterranean influence. Look for wines made from indigenous and international grape varieties, including Nero d'Avola and Chardonnay. The sunny climate and proximity to the sea contribute to the unique character of the wines. And let's say that part again: you are next to the sea!

Alcamo: The Alcamo historic wine region has a strong tradition of winemaking. The Alcamo DOC produces a variety of wines, including both whites and reds. The hilly landscape and maritime climate play a role in the region's wine styles,, and plenty of wineries are ready to welcome you for casual island-vibe tastings and tours.

Palermo and Beyond: In and around the city of the island's capital, Palermo, you can find wine bars and enotecas that offer an array of Sicilian wines for tasting. This is a convenient way to sample a variety of wines from different regions of the island and is a more concentrated area of wine varietals if you are pressed for time on the island or have plans that extend beyond just wineries.

When planning a wine-tasting experience in Sicily, consider exploring these diverse regions to truly appreciate the island's rich wine heritage. Whether you're drawn to Mount Etna's volcanic wines or Marsala's fortified wines, Sicily offers a wine adventure that's as diverse as its landscapes and cultures and a seriously good summer holiday to boot.

## Summary of Chapter 6

In this chapter, we have covered the passion and welcoming nature of the Southern regions of Italy and chose four regions in the South - Campania, Puglia and the islands of Sardinia and Sicily - to explore in depth the world-class wine and finely tuned Italian custom of wine tours and tastings in these areas.

In Campania on the mainland, we looked at the rich and complex red wines such as Taurasi and Aglianico del Taburno, and their profile making the region one of Italy's oldest wine-producing areas. We looked at the best wineries in the region to try the iconic region's grapes, such as Aglianico and Piedrosso, used to make the Costa d'Amalfi DOC wines.

Moving over the region border to Puglia, we addressed how, generally this region is known for being an affordable wine region to explore and do tours, so it is an excellent option in choosing value for quality. Puglia is rightfully known for producing wines with excellent value for their standard, with a fair balance between price and taste and being accessible to many varied wine groups.

We covered Puglia's indigenous grape varieties, including Primitivo, Negroamaro, and Fiano, and how well-suited they are to the region's climate and terroir, leading to cost-effective cultivation and production. To get to see these being produced is to experience Puglia's gorgeous winery scene of family-run, modest wineries with lower expenses, more family-owned traditions and welcoming nature.

On the southern Italian islands of Sardinia and Sicily, the chapter delved into what sets them apart from the mainlands and what experiences you might get here that you otherwise might not on the mainland - such as dedicated wine weeks, bike tour versions and island-vine wine festivals that erupt from local markets to everyone's delight. We looked at the best places on both islands to get your winery fix, what these experiences will look like, and for which groups they might best be suited.

In general, when visiting a more chilled-out Southern Italy and the beautiful islands of Sicily and Sardinia, be sure to come with not only a sunhat, but an open palate and a curious spirit to discover the unique flavours of unusual wines and lesser-known labels. The qualities of wines from these regions are what matters, and a warmer climate and homely environment in which to try them. Enjoy the warm hospitality, learn about wine-making traditions, and savour the beauty of postcard surroundings as you indulge in a memorable wine-tasting experience.. don't try too hard.

*Figure 68. Martini Asti Wine*

CHAPTER 7

# WRAP-UP

I hope you have enjoyed being part of this journey across the wineries of Italy and sharing the options for well-matched wine holidays to suit varied groups. Between us at IloveItaly.wine, as a group of Italian wine-lovers and travellers, we hope that our decades of experience sipping on Italian wine across the country has helped to shape a potential itinerary for your trip. Thanks to additional research on many others we hope to visit very soon, which we have also shared in this book, we have provided as comprehensive an overview as we can of where to go and what to drink!

From the wineries shared in this book, stretching from the far north in Piemonte to the southern islands of Sardinia and Sicily, you can pull together an itinerary to suit all tastes, group sizes and budgets. Remember, you can do as little of the planning of the trip as you like, and we have shared many tour guide companies in each area that can organise everything from your travel, accommodation and tastings or tours - then all you will need to do is turn up on the day and enjoy the wine! Or we hope to have made it very easy to contact each winery directly and organise things yourself if you have the time and bandwidth to do so... It's a welcome distraction from work, let's face it!

Wine-making and enjoying a wine tour holiday in Italy is a captivating and immersive experience that varies from region to region. Still, it always offers a unique blend of cultural learning, the opportunity to connect with Italian traditions, and some seriously good food and wine to go with it.

I hope we have shared the expectations of wine tours, both in group settings or booked directly as an experience yourselves, and what to look for in the vineyards - learning about the grapevines up close and being ready to look for different grape varieties in their terroir (soil, climate, and geography).

Depending on the season, you might have the chance to participate in the grape harvest, and if you love a hands-on experience that allows you to appreciate the labour-intensive process of wine, then I hope you time it well and visit the right winery for you to absorb all stages of harvesting process shared earlier in the book.

When exploring an Italian winery's cellar, enjoy learning about the fermentation tanks, oak barrels, and other equipment used in winemaking - and don't be shy to ask questions of the guides who love to share their knowledge of the winemaking process, from grape crushing to ageing.

Figure 69. Italian Wines

Understanding the science and artistry behind winemaking and what goes on in the cellars adds depth to your appreciation of the final product. It is something special and distinctive to take away from your Italian wine experience.

And finally, enjoy every sip, sniff and swirl in the mouth of the wonderful tasting sessions offered on your wine trip - these are, after all, the highlight of any wine tour. Be sure to sample a variety of wines, grape types and flavours, and branch out to colours and aromas you have perhaps yet to try. There is no better time than to be guided by experts to help you understand the nuances of each wine's aroma, flavour, and structure and build your understanding of wines to bring home and add to your collections.

We hope you meet lovely people along the way, engage in exciting discussions about Italian wines' characteristics, and the history of the wineries, and come to appreciate the cultural significance of wines in the region as much as we have. Learning about wine from experts enhances your knowledge, deepens your connection to the local Italian culture and is often the hook that will draw you back to Italy again and again.

Interacting with winemakers and their teams provides a glimpse into their passion and dedication to the craft that you cannot help but be charmed by. It's an opportunity to ask questions, learn from their expertise, and share their enthusiasm.

A wine tour holiday in Italy offers more than just wine—it creates memories that last a lifetime. The experience of exploring vineyards, learning about winemaking, savouring local Italian cuisine, and connecting with the people behind the wines enriches a love of Italy's cultural heritage and its passionate relationship with wine.

Whether you're a novice or a connoisseur, I hope you have learned what your perfect wine tour holiday in Italy might look like, and endeavour to fulfil a journey of discovery, celebration, tradition and sheer joy in every sip.

**Salute!**

# Please review this book!

If you enjoy this book, we would be so grateful to hear your thoughts! Your reviews are not only a source of motivation for us as authors but also invaluable for other readers looking for their next great read. Sharing your feedback can help us reach more book lovers like you. Please take a moment to leave a short review and share your experience with us, it makes such a huge difference! Thank you for being a part of our wine journey!

# REFERENCES

- *Villa Calcinaia. (n.d.). https://www.conticapponi.it/calci naia/activities/*

- *Antinori Winery & Brolio Castle - Private Tour. (2023, September 9). Viator. https://www.viator.com/en-GB/tours/Florence/Antinori-Winery-and-Brolio-Castle-Private-Tour/d519-132244P19?m=64814&supag=127985999160&supsc=dsa-694098303764&supai=537208497557&supdv=c&supnt=g&suplp=1006561&supli=&supti=dsa-694098303764&tsem=true&supci=dsa-694098303764&supap1=&supap2=&gclid=Cj0KCQjw98ujBhCgARIsAD7QeAj3De8do7-R39iklED5_0XUux6kfuUe7Tb0QZEpZeQXVcmJPT4ETNkaAuJMEALw_wcB*

- *Archer, L., & Archer, L. (2022, November 21). The Green Heart of Italy: Umbria - SOMM TV Magazine. SOMM TV Magazine - A World of Wine, Food & Travel. https://mag.sommtv.com/2022/11/umbria-wine-region/*

- *Arnaldo Caprai. (2023, July 5). Arnaldo Caprai. The Sagrantino di Montefalco. Arnaldo Caprai - Sagrantino*

Di Montefalco. https://www.arnaldocaprai.it/en/

- Aveine. (2021, December 17). *All about amphora wine - Aveine - Blog*. Aveine - Blog. https://www.aveine.paris/blog/en/all-about-amphora-wine/

- Aveine. (2022, May 18). *Overview of the Wine culture in Italy - Aveine - Blog*. Aveine - Blog. https://www.aveine.paris/blog/en/overview-of-the-wine-culture-in-italy/

- Banfi. (n.d.). *Banfi - Sustainability*. Banfi. https://www.banfi.it/en/sustainability/

- *Bellavista wine online. Bellavista winery (Italy) on Uritalianwines*. (n.d.). NegozioDelVino. https://www.uritalianwines.com/bellavista-B59.htm

- Cantina Li Duni. (2023, March 9). *Cantina Li Duni - The sea wines. Vines ungrafted Badesi*. Cantina Li Duni - Gallura Wines. https://www.cantinaliduni.it/en/

- *Cantine Barbera | Organic Vineyard &amp; Winery in Menfi, Sicily*. (n.d.). Cantine Barbera - Vini Menfi Sicilia. https://www.cantinebarbera.it/en/

- *Cantine due palme*. (n.d.). https://www.cantineduepalme.wine/en/

- Capalbo, C., & Capalbo, C. (2020). *Southern Italy for wine lovers: Wineries and vineyard stays*. Decanter. https://www.decanter.com/wine-travel/southern-it

aly-wineries-vineyard-stays-434926/

- *Caserta Royal Palace and Park, Italy | World Heritage Journeys of Europe. (n.d.). https://visitworldheritage.com/en/eu/caserta-royal-palace-and-park-italy/73cf1988-9d13-4658-99f5-2f23a706bc00*

- *Central Italy. (n.d.). Italy Review. https://www.italyreview.com/central-italy.html*

- *Climate and Geology di Langhe e Roero - Consorzio Barolo e Barbaresco. (2022, August 1). Consorzio Di Tutela Barolo Barbaresco Alba Langhe E Dogliani. https://www.langhevini.it/en/the-territory/climate/*

- *Company | Marchesi di Barolo. (n.d.). https://marchesibarolo.com/en/company*

- *Di Filippo Wines. (2022, February 8). Di Filippo Wines. Di Filippo Wines | Organic Wines in Umbria. https://vinidifilippo.com/en/*

- *Ducker, J., & Ducker, J. (2023). Le Marche wineries to visit. Decanter. https://www.decanter.com/wine-travel/italy/le-marche-wineries-to-visit-387435/?gad=1&gclid=Cj0KCQjw5f2lBhCkARIsAHeTvlhncj_5MvNJb34ujiqLbRGVmCMWCQeGw7-demgZP0vl_S_ocxqiOYUaAl5uEALw_wcB*

- *Fatalone Primitivo Gioia del Colle 2021 - Noble Green.*

(n.d.). https://noblegreenwines.co.uk/products/fatalone-primitivo-gioia-del-colle-d65aafb1-399f-4b35-9d34-865e81f2de39

- Fawkes, H., & Fawkes, H. (2023). Top Tuscan wineries: Ten to visit. Decanter. https://www.decanter.com/wine-travel/top-10-tuscan-wineries-to-visit-13770/2/

- Feudi di San Gregorio. (n.d.). Feudi Di San Gregorio. https://www.feudi.it/en

- Florio hospitality, the guided tour of the Winery in Marsala. (n.d.). Duca Di Salaparuta. https://www.duca.it/en/florio/ospitalita/

- Frappato Vittoria D.O.C. | Planeta Winery. (n.d.). Planeta Winery. https://planeta.it/en/wine/frappato-en/

- Frescobaldi Winery at Castello Nipozzano, Wine tasting in Tuscany, Italy. (n.d.). https://www.summerinitaly.com/guide/frescobaldi-winery-at-castello-nipozzano

- GAJA - Barolo and Barbaresco Wine Tours and Tastings - all wine tours. (2022, January 12). All Wine Tours. https://allwinetours.com/wineries/gaja/

- GAJA - Wilson Daniels. (2023, July 21). Wilson Daniels. https://wilsondaniels.com/winery/gaja/

- Gaja in Tuscany with Gaia and Angelo Gaja. (n.d.). Wine Spectator. https://www.winespectator.com/video/play/id/NUrpiFlc/title/gaja-in-tuscany-with-gaia-and-angelo-gaja

- *Guided Wine Tours Florence Tuscany | Grape Tours | Italy. (n.d.). Grape Tours.* https://www.tuscan-wine-tours.com/

- *Hellobarrio. (2020, May 14). Azienda Agricola Azelia, 100 anni di storia grazie a cinque generazioni. Azelia.* https://www.azelia.it/

- *Hellobarrio. (2021). Visite in cantina dove nascono i grandi vini delle Langhe. Villaggio Narrante in Fontanafredda & Casa Di E. Mirafiore.* https://www.villaggionarrante.it/cantine/visite-in-cantina/

- *I Pastini srl - Produzione vini Puglia. (n.d.).* https://www.ipastini.it/

- *Italy. (n.d.).* https://www.abercrombiekent.co.uk/destinations/europe/italy

- *Just Sicily | Festivals and Events in Sicily | What's Going On, Sicily Festivals, Sicily Events, Festivals in Sicily, Events in Sicily, Events Happening in Sicily, Festivals in Sicily in March, Festivals in Sicily in April, Festivals in Sicily in May, Festivals in Sicily in June, Festivals in Sicily in July, Festivals in Sicily in August, Festivals in Sicily in September, Festivals in Sicily in October, San Giorgio, Windsurfing Festival at Mondello, Milazzo Castle, Almond Blossom Festival, Santa Agata, Carnevale, Tyridaris, Festival of St Joseph, Incyon Wine Festival, Pesce* a Mare, Cantine Aperte, Pasqua, The Procession of Mysteries, Sagra del Lago, Nivarata,, Infiorata, Estate Ennese, Festival of St Rosalia, Stragusto. Boat Race Ortigia, Ferragosta, Caccarrio, Monte Pellegino, Couscous Festival. (n.d.). https://www.justsicily.co.uk/pages/festivals-and-events-in-sicily/#:~:text=Sicilian%20festivals%20are%20usually%20religious,the%20Greek%20Theatre%20in%20Taormina

- Kimmelman, M. (2013, August 26). Archea Architects' headquarters for Antinori winemakers. The New York Times. https://www.nytimes.com/2013/08/27/arts/design/archea-architects-headquarters-for-antinori-winemakers.html

- Luther, E. V. (2022). The Italian Wine Connoisseur (1st ed.) [Paperback]. Monogram Publishers.

- Mapdev. (2022, December 27). Ciù Ciù Tenimenti Bartolomei - vini italiani di qualità. www.ciuciutenimenti.it. https://www.ciuciutenimenti.it/

- marketing-content. (2016, August 25). What to do in an emergency during your trip to Italy - Italy Now. Italy Now. https://italynow.com/blog/emergency-trip-italy/

- Meet Piemonte. (2022, May 26). Piedmont Wine Tour Vacation | 6 days, 5 nights. https://meetpiemonte.com/en/tour/wine-tours/piedmont-wine-tour-vacation

- Meet Piemonte. (2023, July 14). Grand Tour of Tuscany |

Small-group tour of Italy | Stay in a Tuscan Villa. https://meetpiemonte.com/en/tour/grand-tour-of-tuscany

- *Palazzone. (2023, June 1). Cantina Palazzone Orvieto. https://www.palazzone.com/*

- *Piemonte, M. (2023). The Piedmont region of Italy. Meet Piemonte. https://meetpiemonte.com/en/blog/the-piedmont-region-of-italy*

- *Rosemary, Rosemary, & Rosemary. (2023). A guide to the Prosecco Road – Italy’s bubbliest secret. Rosemary and Pork Belly. https://rosemaryandporkbelly.co.uk/prosecco-road-veneto-italy/*

- *Spoleto Best food & Wine Travel Guide | Truffles Scorzone | Grechetto. (n.d.). https://www.trips2italy.com/umbria/spoleto-food-wine.html*

- *Stark, A. (2020). A sommelier's guide to Lazio Wine — La Vita Roma. La Vita Roma. https://www.lavitaroma.com/blog/lazio-wine-guide*

- *Team, D. I. (2022). Wine tasting in Gallura. Copyright (C) 2000 - 2023 Delicious Italy. https://www.deliciousitaly.com/sardinia-food-wine/wine-tasting-in-gallura#:~:text=Wine%20Tastings%20at%20Capichera%20Winery&text=Lasting%2090%20to%20120%20minutes,territory%20to%20accompany%20each%20label.*

- *Team, D. I. (2023). A Gallura Wine route. Copyright (C) 2000 - 2023 Delicious Italy. https://www.deliciousitaly.com/sardinia-food-wine/a-gallura-wine-route*

- *The Wine Bus - your Italian food and wine tour. (n.d.). https://www.thewinebus.net/tours*

- *TimeMaps. (2022, September 5). Etruscans: Civilization, history and Influence on Rome | TimeMaps. https://timemaps.com/civilizations/etruscans/?utm_content=cmp-true*

- *Tour and tasting of the Castle in the Chianti Classico. (n.d.). https://wineclub.castellomeleto.it/en/shop/le-esperienze/tour-of-the-castle-with-wine-tasting/*

- *Tripadvisor. (2023, July 12). 2023 Winery tour and private tasting in Montefalco. https://www.tripadvisor.co.uk/AttractionProductReview-g608939-d22680101-Winery_Tour_and_Private_Tasting_in_Montefalco-Montefalco_Province_of_Perugia_Umbri.html*

- *ttAdmin, & ttAdmin. (2022). From vineyard to cellar. Tuscany Tonight. https://tuscanytonight.com/From-Vineyard-to-Cellar*

- *Valsecchi, C. (2023). Prosecco or franciacorta. Lake Como for You. https://lakecomoforyou.com/prosecco-or-franciacorta/*

- *Vinilla Wine Resort, castle hotel in Manduria, Puglia. (*

- n.d.). https://www.viniliaresort.com/en/luxury-resort-in-the-castle-manduria

- *Wine Tour in Tuscany – Wine Tour in Tuscany – wine tasting tours in Florence / Siena, Chianti, Montalcino, San Gimignano, Montepulciano, Tuscany, Italy.* (n.d.). https://www.winetourintuscany.com/

- *WineTourism.com.* (n.d.-a). *10 best wine tours & tastings in Umbria 2023.* https://www.winetourism.com/wine-tasting-tours-in-umbria/

- *WineTourism.com.* (n.d.-b). *10 best wineries in Campania to visit in 2023.* https://www.winetourism.com/wineries-in-campania-wine-region/

- *WineTourism.com.* (n.d.-c). *Cantine Gabriele Palmas - winery in Sardinia | Winetourism.com.* https://www.winetourism.com/winery/cantine-gabriele-palmas/

- *WineTourism.com.* (n.d.-d). *Castello di Corbara - Winery in Umbria | Winetourism.com.* https://www.winetourism.com/winery/castello-di-corbara/

- *WineTourism.com.* (n.d.-e). *D'Antiche Terre - winery in Campania | Winetourism.com.* https://www.winetourism.com/winery/dantiche-terre/

- *WineTourism.com.* (n.d.-f). *Le Vigne di Raito - winery in Campania | Winetourism.com.* https://www.winetourism.com/winery/le-vigne-di-raito/

- *WineTourism.com. (n.d.-g). Mastroberardino - winery in Campania | Winetourism.com.* https://www.winetourism.com/winery/mastroberardino/

- *WineTourism.com. (n.d.-h). Montecucco - wine region in Tuscany, Italy | winetourism.com.* https://www.winetourism.com/wine-appellation/montecucco/#:~:text=The%20Montecucco%20wine%20region%20is%20in%20the%20warm%20southern%20corner,di%20Montalcino%20to%20the%20northeast.

- *WineTourism.com. (n.d.-i). Top wine regions to visit in Italy 2023.* https://www.winetourism.com/wine-country/italy/

- *Zetabi. (n.d.). Monsordo Bernardina Estate - Ceretto Aziende vitivinicole.* https://www.ceretto.com/en//tenuta-monsordo-bernardina

www.ingramcontent.com/pod-product-compliance
Lightning Source LLC
Chambersburg PA
CBHW052133070526
44585CB00017B/1810